CHILDREN'S RIGHTS

CHILDREN'S RIGHTS

Today's Global Challenge

John Wall

ROWMAN & LITTLEFIELD
Lanham • Boulder • New York • London

Published by Rowman & Littlefield
A wholly owned subsidiary of
The Rowman & Littlefield Publishing Group, Inc.
4501 Forbes Boulevard, Suite 200, Lanham, Maryland 20706
https://rowman.com

Unit A, Whitacre Mews, 26-34 Stannary Street, London SE11 4AB,
United Kingdom

British Library Cataloguing in Publication Information Available

Library of Congress Cataloging-in-Publication Data
Names: Wall, John, 1965– author.
Title: Children's rights : today's global challenge / John Wall.
Description: Lanham : Rowman & Littlefield, [2017] | Includes bibliographical
    references and index.
Identifiers: LCCN 2016033705 (print) | LCCN 2016037456 (ebook) | ISBN
    9781442249776 (hardcover : alk. paper) | ISBN 9781442249837 (pbk. : alk.
    paper) | ISBN 9781442249783 (electronic)
Subjects: LCSH: Children's rights. | Child labor. | Child slaves. | Children—
    Legal status, laws, etc.
Classification: LCC HQ789 .W35 2017 (print) | LCC HQ789 (ebook) | DDC
    323.3/52—dc23
LC record available at https://lccn.loc.gov/2016033705

Printed in the United States of America

CONTENTS

I

WHY CHILDREN'S RIGHTS

Tazim Ali is the nine-year-old president of the children's parliament in the ancient limestone city of Varanasi, India. The children's parliament, started in the 1990s and meeting every Sunday, has succeeded in changing local laws on a variety of issues: lack of accessible health services, police brutality toward working children, sexual abuse by teachers, harassment of girls, access for disabled children, street lighting, and much else.

Ali was elected for a one-year term and has become known across Varanasi for quickly responding to calls on his cell phone and pressuring the city's adult politicians to act. "I was called recently because a 2-year-old girl didn't have enough food. She ended up dying," he said. "We can get people to pay attention to us. We brought the case to the police. They saw we were serious and didn't want to turn children away."[1] Like children and youth in the thirty or so other countries around the world that have children's parliaments, Ali and his fellow elected parliamentarians are showing that, given the chance, young people are able to stand up for their rights.

Children and youth under the age of eighteen constitute a third of all humanity. However, until recently, few believed that they should have any rights at all. Indeed, as we will see, the modern idea of rights, as created in the Enlightenment, explicitly carved out a public space for adults only (indeed, initially only wealthy white men). Rights existed outside the private sphere of the home to govern a supposedly "rational" public sphere in which minors were not thought in any way competent to participate.

As a result, when we think about human rights today, we tend to think first and foremost about adults. Children and youth are often assumed to have rights only in a derivative or secondhand way. Of course, other groups, like women, the poor, and ethnic minorities, have had to fight for their rights over history too. They have had to prove that they are equal public citizens. But children and child advocates face an especially daunting task. They have to overcome the very foundation of modern rights as a sphere for the privileges of adulthood.

At the same time, most people today would acknowledge that children and youth do and should in fact have quite a lot of rights. Few would deny that children have rights, for example, not to be sexually abused, done violence to, or discriminated against. Or that they have basic rights to an education, food security, and health care. Or that they have at least some rights to freedom of expression, political participation, and assembly. Of course, having rights may be different from enjoying them in reality. And the rights one has may vary greatly in different contexts, countries, and cultures. But it is difficult to argue anymore that children simply are not owed any rights at all.

This book is a comprehensive exploration of both the ambiguities and the promise of the children's rights movement. It examines the children's rights movement on different levels of theory, history, and practice. Theoretically, it looks at how to understand what it could mean for children to have rights in the first place and how children's rights might be related to larger human rights. Historically, it examines the worldwide struggles that have taken place over children's rights over the past two centuries. And practically, it digs down into some of the major children's rights controversies taking place around the world today.

It will turn out that children's rights are arguably the major human rights challenge of the twenty-first century. They are fundamental to the most significant issues of our time: from poverty to education, health care to war, and cultural conflict to climate change. But even more important, children's rights are the greatest remaining frontier in humanity's experiment in human rights as such. In a century, we will likely look back on today's attitudes about children's rights the same way we now look back on attitudes about women's and minorities' rights a century ago. We will see how profoundly young people are treated as second-class citizens in our time. This is the century of children's rights.

For these reasons, a critical examination of children's rights is also a critical examination of human rights. I refer to this broader effort as "childism." Childism is a term that is analogous to feminism, womanism, queer theory, environmentalism, and other methods for overcoming historical prejudice. Childism seeks to transform ideas and societies in response to the particular lived experiences of children. In terms of human rights, it tries to imagine how they can be understood and practiced in creative new ways that are fully inclusive of children.[2]

From a childist perspective, the children's rights movement challenges societies not only to give children the same rights as adults, but, in a more profound way, to change the meaning of rights themselves. Children will be included in human rights only when human rights are thought about and enacted in ways that respond to children and adults equally. Childism is another kind of critique of patriarchy—or rule by the "pater" or father—now in terms not of its sexism but of its adultism, its historically ingrained biases in favor of people who think of themselves as adults. These biases simply assume, often in unseen ways, that some definition of "adulthood" is the true model and standard of "humanity." The aim through childism is for human rights to overcome their traditional adult-centrism and thereby become more fully, complexly, and meaningfully human.

Rights have been critiqued in terms of gender, ethnicity, race, class, and sexuality. These efforts have met with much success but also have far to go. It is now time to critique rights also in terms of age. Can we start to think about human rights in new ways that include children and youth fully? Can our laws and policies respond to children's issues as equally important to adults'? Can children and youth acquire what the philosopher Hannah Arendt calls "the right to have rights" as first-class rather than second-class citizens?

Building on scholarship and activism in children's rights, the following chapters suggest that the key transformation needed is for children's rights to focus less on "child saving" and more on "child empowerment."

Child saving is the assumption that children's rights exist primarily as means for children to be taken care of by adults: to be protected from various kinds of violence and harm and to be provided with various kinds of entitlements and resources. These ways in which adults take responsibility for children are certainly important. But they reduce children only to human rights objects, denying them opportunities also to act as human rights subjects.

Child empowerment, in contrast, means that children's rights are founded on a deeper respect for children as equally important contributors to societies. Just as for adults, rights to protections and provisions do not have to exclude rights to participation. Rather, in whatever new and imaginative ways would be necessary, children need and deserve to be included as fully empowered members of the human rights community.

Children's rights are a concern not only for scholars but also for anyone who works with, cares about, or lives alongside children. That is, it is a concern for us all. We all live alongside children in every aspect of our lives, whether immediately in families, schools, and child-related professions, or indirectly through local communities, shared societies, and global interconnections.

This book is written especially for students and researchers in any field dealing with children, including childhood studies, history, sociology, anthropology, psychology, literature, philosophy, religion, public policy, and law. It is also targeted toward professionals and practitioners who work with children in non-governmental organizations (NGOs), government agencies, education, social work, therapy, law, or medicine. And finally, I hope this book will be of interest to anyone who wants to think critically and imaginatively about human rights, social justice, and creating a better world for us all.

Tazim Ali and all the world's 2.3 billion children deserve full and equal inclusion in the sphere of human rights.[3] They should be not only seen but also heard. No era can systematically deprive a sector of humanity of its rights without also depriving humanity of its own humanity.

WHY CHILDREN?

There is no single definition of "children." The term has different meanings across diverse cultures and societies, both historically and today. It can refer either to actual people ("children") or to socially constructed ideas about those people ("childhoods"). In addition, it is possible to make different kinds of distinction, or no distinction at all, between infants, children, adolescents, youth, young people, adults, the elderly, and so on.

In order to provide some focus for our discussions, on the whole this book uses a relatively expansive definition of "children" and "childhood" to refer to anyone under the age of eighteen. This is the definition generally used by the United Nations, the major international body concerned with human rights. So defined, children constitute approximately a third of all human beings on the planet, with the other two thirds being women and men, respectively. In recognition of the plasticity of the term, I will use the term "children" more or less interchangeably with similar terms like "children and youth" and "young people."

Childhood, however, is not just a simple matter of biological age. It is also an idea that is historically and culturally constructed. For example, while most Americans assume today that children are born quite incompetent and dependent, in the nineteenth century American children led significantly more independent lives from very early ages and were considered adults sooner. And elsewhere in the world, such as among the Beng of West Africa, the assumption today is that infants are reincarnations of past lives bringing great spiritual knowledge and ready to lead largely independent lives from their parents once they can walk.[4] Childhood can also be defined less by age than by status, in many cultures marriage, in which case it could equally end at nine as at fifty-nine years of age.

Because childhood means different things in different times and places, there is not really one "childhood" but rather many "childhoods." Likewise, those who like to think of themselves as "adults" are really using a socially constructed category for which there are many different possible "adulthoods." Sometimes the category "adults" helps to marginalize "children" by creating a rigid binary opposition between human groups. It can contribute to consolidating adult power. On the other hand, the categories of "child" and "adult" can also prove useful for identifying and understanding a neglected group.

Let us start by asking why one would pay attention to the rights specifically of children. There are at least three basic reasons.

First and most broadly, children today are the world's most disadvantaged group.

While we are used to combatting biases of sexism, classism, and racism, the world has yet to confront with equal seriousness the implicit and explicit ways in which all societies and cultures engage in systemic biases of adultism.

But the facts speak for themselves. Children across the world are more likely than adults to be poor, malnourished, deprived of security, prevented from exercising freedoms, silenced, done violence, abused, exploited, and discriminated against. Of course, many children in many contexts are treated with great dignity and respect. Many are better off than adults and receive significant societal resources. But when it comes to how people are treated on average, young people face unique depths of structural injustice. Children are sometimes placed on an ethereal pedestal of innocence only thereby to be ignored as subjects of serious public concern.

Take, for example, child poverty. In almost every country in the world, rich or poor, the younger you happen to be, the more likely you are to be poor. Age is usually a greater predictor of poverty than gender, race, or ethnicity. Half the world's current children live below their country's line of poverty. UNICEF estimates that "the majority of children in developing countries are suffering from severe [economic] deprivation."[5] In wealthy countries, babies are typically the poorest group, followed by children and then youth. For example, the poverty rate of newborns through seventeen-year-olds in the United States is currently 23 percent while the overall poverty rate is 19 percent. Even in the United Kingdom, estimated to have the strongest combination in any country of public and private resources for children, child poverty still stands at 12 percent compared with overall poverty of 10 percent.[6]

Children need greater consideration of their rights, therefore, because they are, generally speaking, more profoundly disadvantaged than are adults.

The second reason it is important to consider the rights specifically of children is that children's lives have shifted radically in the past few decades, from the public realm usually associated with rights into the private realm of home and school, where rights are often more contested.

This historic shift is taking place just as other groups, such as women and minorities, have moved in the opposite direction, from private sequestering toward greater public standing. Sometimes these two trends are directly related: previously excluded adults gaining public rights on the grounds that they should no longer be treated like children. Of course, the reality is that children and youth very much exist in the public sphere as well. They are health resource users, legal persons, market consumers, affected by political policies, and in general citizens deserving societal dignity and respect. But what the political theorist Iris Marion Young says about women is even more true for children: "No persons, actions, or aspects of a person's life should be forced into privacy."[7] Children and youth are now the largest segment of society that is "forced into privacy" because they are the most likely group to be denied public status and visibility and hence public rights.

Take the example with which this chapter began. It may seem surprising that a nine-year-old could contribute usefully to public policy debates. But in reality, there have always been children and youth who have stood up for their public rights, and there are children and youth doing so all over the world today. Think about Malala Yousafzai, the Pakistani youth who won the Nobel Prize fighting for girls' rights to education. Young people fought on the front lines with their mothers in struggles for women's suffrage; marched with Gandhi against British colonial rule in India; played active parts in civil rights actions such as school integration in the United States; and much more. Children today are active in social movements ranging from animal rights to antigenocide campaigns and fighting global warming.

Part of the difficulty facing children's rights is therefore a deepening privatization, indeed romanticization, of childhood that makes it more difficult to imagine children as full rights-holding public citizens.

And third, the rights of children have become particularly problematic in today's era of rapid globalization.

Globalization can be defined as the increasing interconnectedness of persons across the planet through economics, technology, and culture. These processes, as we will see in the next chapter, are weakening the role of nation-states in protecting and advancing human rights. They are strengthening the power of supernational agencies such as global corporations and mass media. Globalization has been occurring for centuries, but in the past fifty to sixty years it has accelerated to a point where long-standing rights guarantees are increasingly under threat.

Under globalization, children and youth find themselves even more systematically disadvantaged than they would otherwise be. They are on the whole more likely than adults to be exploited by global marketplaces and technologies and disempowered by global orders of governance. This is not to say that children and youth are not also finding new avenues of self-empowerment, such as ways to earn a living, speak up for themselves online, and organize with others across local borders. And of course a number of global non-governmental organizations have arisen to promote children's rights in areas such as health care, literacy, education, and disaster relief. However, on the whole, globalization poses more challenges for those groups like children who already have less power to begin with.

Consider, for example, today's worldwide growth in child slavery. We will examine this phenomenon in detail in chapter 5. Contrary to popular belief, child slavery is not confined to the world's poorest countries and has arguably increased in recent decades. The International Labour Organization (ILO) estimates that there are currently more than five million children working in slave conditions around the world, such as in factories, agriculture, domestic servitude, prostitution, pornography, organized crime, or drug trafficking.

On the one hand, global technologies and non-governmental organizations make the experiences of child slaves known to the world and have helped to fight against it. On the other hand, global corporations and international criminal organizations are able to evade local and national efforts to erase child slavery with increasing ease. Despite slavery being illegal in every country in the world, global actors can move exploitative workplaces and exploited people across borders. And they can pressure and bribe local officials to tolerate abusive work conditions in the name of local economic gain.

As a result, the Dickensian era of child labor that ushered in the modern children's rights movement in the nineteenth century is now back and with something of a vengeance. The clothes you are currently wearing and the food you ate for breakfast are likely to have benefitted from the labor exploitation of children even if invisibly and from great distances.

In these and other ways, children today need renewed and more creative attention paid to their rights. Rights do not solve every social problem. But at the same time, few of us would be happy not to have them. When it comes to children, their disadvantages, privatization, and global disempowerment call out for improved children's rights and new forms of human rights community. It is time for human rights to take more seriously the many-sided challenges of age.

WHY RIGHTS?

If children face special difficulties in today's world, why confront those difficulties using concepts and practices of rights?

There are many other ways to address children's, as well as adults', issues. We could be speaking instead of children's needs, development, or flourishing. We could examine broader questions of community, society, or culture. All of these are related to questions of children's rights. But why focus on rights specifically?

There are three basic reasons to focus specifically on children's rights.

First, children's rights already *are* important parts of conversations about children's lives around the world.

Ever since the United Nations' landmark 1989 Convention on the Rights of the Child (CRC)—an international treaty that we will discuss in detail later on, and the most widely ratified treaty in all of history—children's rights have become the *de facto* global language for dealing with the concerns of children. Not all people or cultures accept or even acknowledge that children have rights. And the very notion of rights has arguably problematic roots in Western individualism. But one would be hard pressed to find another social framework today that has gained such universal standing. Almost every legal system on the planet is built upon rights, so that even in this legal sense, rights are the backbone of child-related public policy. For example, it is a legal right in almost every country in the world for children not to be sexually abused. And beyond just law, few would argue that children do not have moral rights to be treated with dignity and respect.

Let us take the highly controversial example of female genital cutting (FGC). The World Health Organization defines FGC (also known as female genital mutilation, or FGM) as "all procedures that involve partial or total removal of the external female genitalia or other injury to the female genital organs for non-medical reasons."[8] The practice ranges from nicking or burning the clitoris to the partial or total removal of the clitoris or the removal of the external genitalia altogether. Of the 125 million females around the world who are currently estimated to have undergone FGC, about half were circumcised before the age of five and the other half between five and puberty.

While FGC can be thought about using a variety of non-rights languages—such as those of medical and psychological health, respect for traditional cultures, and consequences pro and con for girls' future marital prospects and economic security—it is almost impossible not to consider as well issues of children's rights. For one thing, FGC has now been legally banned by the United Nations, the African Union, and most countries. For another, it is an issue of moral rights: whether civil rights to protection against violence and discrimination or cultural rights allowing girls to become marriageable and avoid a life of poverty and childlessness.

In issues like FGC, failing to understand the human rights dimensions means failing to understand important parts of contemporary debates about children's lives.

Second, it is also important to focus on children's rights because doing so brings into clearer focus children's shared humanity.

Few would argue that we should not talk about rights when it comes to adults. Rights provide adults with a common sense of human dignity. Indeed, adults have fought and died for a large number of rights over hundreds, if not thousands, of years. Few adults would voluntarily give up their rights, for example, to non-discrimination, non-abuse, relief aid, freedom of speech, freedom of conscience, and so on. It may turn out to be the case that some adult rights are not appropriate for children or not in quite the same way, or that some children's rights are not appropriate for adults. It may be that some child and adult rights vary by cultural context. But this does not mean that the language of rights should not have just as much importance in children's lives as it does in adults'. Indeed, since adults generally have more power and rights than children, the rights of children need greater rather than less consideration.

Human rights on the whole are the kinds of things that everyone should have on some level, regardless of people's many kinds of differences. Children's rights are human rights.

An example here is children's migration rights. Tens of thousands of children migrate alone every year across borders, whether to join families, to escape war or persecution, or to find work and educational opportunities. But receiving countries often treat minors differently from adults. For example, minors may be denied family reunion rights, incarcerated without due process rights, or deported without rights to be heard.[9] This kind of double standard can be illuminated and challenged by shining the spotlight of human rights on children's equal needs with those of adults to be treated with dignity, respect, and humanity.

Third and finally, discussion of children's lives in terms of rights is important for a broader reason, which is to think about what it could mean for all of us to live in a more just society.

Not only are all of us children at some point in our lives, but even when we are no longer children, we share our world with children. This common world remains distorted if children's rights are ignored within it. Child and youth rights are part of the long historical struggle for justice and fairness. It is like the situation in George Orwell's *Animal Farm* in which the pigs declare that all animals are equal, but some animals are more equal than others. In the long historical struggle for social justice, societies have had to learn over and over again that a just world cannot be built on unjust foundations. Slavery makes the entire public economy corrupt. Sexism debases men as well as women. In the same way, denying children rights diminishes and distorts the human rights community itself. It dehumanizes not only childhood but also adulthood. It prevents both adults and children from living full and just lives.

There are different ways to bring new groups into the world of human rights. Those groups can be provided only the rights that dominant groups allow them. They can fight to have the same rights that dominant groups already enjoy. But the historical reality is that previously marginalized groups only gain their full human rights insofar as the very idea of "human rights" expands in new ways to include them. Take, for example, women gaining rights in the 1970s against physical and sexual abuse. Women here were not simply provided the same rights previously afforded to men. Rather, the very meaning of rights had to shift from largely public protections to include protections in the previously off-limits private realm as well. The personal had to become political.

An example of children's rights challenging broader human rights could be the case of health insurance rights in the United States. Currently these rights come in two major forms: rights to private health insurance through employment, and rights to public health insurance through poverty, disability, or old age. But both these avenues disadvantage children compared to adults, since children can gain private insurance only indirectly if they happen to have a sufficiently employed parent, and they can gain public insurance (unlike the elderly) only if they are sufficiently poor or disabled. The only way that children would no longer suffer from disproportionately less health insurance would be if health insurance rights were restructured for all. This might mean a fully public system that guarantees health insurance rights to everyone or perhaps a public-private system in which children at least enjoy equal rights with the elderly.

A similar reimagination of what it means to have rights has accompanied every expansion of rights throughout history, whether to include not just nobility but also commoners, not just ethnic majorities but also minorities, not just men but also women, not just heterosexuals but also sexual minorities, not just humans but also animals, and so on. The same kind of shift in meaning is now starting to take place as human rights increasingly respond to children. But the world has a long way to go before it includes children equally and fully.

THE CHALLENGE

Children's rights are, consequently, "today's global challenge" in two related senses.

First, children's rights are a challenge *for* the world. Children and youth are the most disadvantaged third of humanity. Their struggles, well-being, and empowerment are in need of significantly greater attention from all of us: students, professionals, activists, policymakers, and concerned citizens alike. The idea that children should have rights is relatively new in history, and the work of formulating and enacting those rights has only just begun.

And second, children's rights are a challenge *to* the world. They can be realized only insofar as societies critique and reform themselves. Children's rights are challenges to everything from national histories to cultural norms and moral and legal practices. They demand that we become more aware of our own implicit adultist biases and develop more inclusive ways of living together. The challenge of children's rights does not concern just children. It concerns even more basically what it means to have human rights in the first place.

The next two chapters look at these challenges in broad terms. Chapter 2 explores rights theory, from its modernist origins to its postmodernist variations, in order to deconstruct its inner adult biases and reconstruct it to include children. Chapter 3 unpacks children's rights in their actual historical development from nineteenth-century child-saving movements to twentieth-century child protections and recent advances in children's rights to public participation.

The three chapters after that dig down into particular examples of children's rights controversies today. They are meant simply to illustrate some of the many basic issues that can be explored. Chapter 4 takes a look at children's rights to an education, examining questions such as whether it is a right at all, whether it should be universal and equal, what it is actually a right to, and how much it should include children's rights to make their own educational choices. Chapter 5 turns to children's rights to be protected against slavery, asking why child slavery persists, how it is changing under globalization, what is meant by protection against exploitation, and how rights language offers solutions. And chapter 6 develops my own reflections on the controversial issue of children's rights to participate in voting, delving into questions of competence, knowledge, and independence as well as potential harms and benefits to children, adults, and societies.

The challenge overall is how the long struggle for human rights can finally include children as children.

2

THEORETICAL CONTROVERSIES

Mary Costin is an eight-year-old with leukemia being treated at a metropolitan medical center in the United States. The childhood studies scholar and anthropologist Myra Bluebond-Langner is talking with Costin in her hospital room. "Are those crayons for me?" Costin asks. "They are for you to use if you want to draw," replies Bluebond-Langner. "Are they new?" "Yes." "OK. Then I'll do a picture for my mother." They draw some flowers and then color in some paper dolls. "They look the way I used to look," Costin comments on the dolls. "Oh." "Yeah, when I had hair." The next morning they talk about what to do with the paper dolls. Costin says: "Put them in their graves, in the Kleenex box. Let me do it. Bring it over here. . . . I'm burying them (*carefully arranges each doll between two sheets of Kleenex*)."[1]

As Bluebond-Langner points out in her pioneering studies of dying children, children like Costin know a great deal more about their life prospects than either their parents or their doctors think they know. Many children not only know they are dying but collude in not discussing their death in order to protect the feelings of their parents and doctors. "All the leukemic children whom I studied faced death with a great deal of understanding about the world of the seriously ill and their place in it. They knew the institution and the disease as well as any lay adult. . . . [T]he terminally ill children [also] knew they were dying before death became imminent. . . . [T]hey kept such knowledge a secret . . . [as active members] of a social order that could only be preserved through the practice of mutual pretense."[2] In Costin's case, she was able to reveal this knowledge to an outside researcher even though her parents made every possible effort to isolate her from other children dying around her.

Costin's situation raises many questions of rights.

On a basic level, what rights does she have to health-care treatment at all? What rights does she have to receive health-care information? Should children have rights to equal or even higher levels of medical treatment as adults?

In addition, should children have rights to informed consent? Should Costin be able to participate in decisions about her own treatment? Are such rights universal or contingent on factors like age and competency? Do they include rights to terminate treatment, try experimental procedures, and determine one's own manner of death?

What about costs? Given scarce medical resources, is Costin owed a right only to a basic level of care or to the best care possible? If a child's parents cannot afford the needed health care, should all children have rights to public assistance? Ought children like Costin to have a right to affordable hospice care or home nursing in their final days? Do they have rights to a good death?

Finally, to what extent are children owed health provisions that are free of racial, gender, class, and other kinds of discrimination? Do terminally and nonterminally ill children have rights to special accommodations in school and communities? Should they have a more general right not to be marginalized by a society that cannot acknowledge that children die?

How one answers these and other children's rights questions depends to a great extent on what one thinks it means to have rights in the first place. It was only a couple of centuries ago that rights began to be thought about as belonging to children at all. There are still thinkers, activists, and policymakers who view "children's rights" as a contradiction in terms. Or who believe that giving children rights undermines rather than enhances children's well-being.

Were Costin an adult, there would be little dispute that she is owed a wide range of medical, social, civic, choice, and other kinds of health-care rights. But because she is a child, her rights fall into more complex kinds of dispute. It is generally easier in contemporary societies to understand what it means for adults to have rights than for children.

This chapter explores the basic question of how, if at all, children's rights can be theoretically understood. This question is basic to the entire study of children's rights. It needs to be explored first so that more concrete controversies can be properly considered. It also implies a number of further questions: what does it mean for anyone to have rights in the first place? Why were rights historically barred to children and youth (as well as, initially, women, minorities, the poor, and others)? Are young people's rights based on the same or different justifications as the rights of adults? Are some theories of rights more child friendly than others? And does including children in rights mean that rights themselves have to be thought about in new ways?

All of these questions are currently in dispute. Taken seriously, they challenge us to reexamine our most fundamental assumptions about what it means for human beings to have the kinds of things we call rights. Because rights theory has historically been meant only for adults, this chapter first examines the reasons for this adultism within the origins of modern rights theory in the Enlightenment. Then we explore the three most influential theoretical frameworks that govern theories of rights today and examine their pros and cons when it comes to the young. Finally, we ask what human rights might look like, theoretically speaking, if they were to avoid their traditional ageism altogether and respond to children's lives equally and fully.

WHY HAVE ADULTS BEEN PRIORITIZED?

If someone asked you *why* you have rights, it would turn out to be a surprisingly difficult question to answer. Because you are human? But not all humans have the same rights. Plus, rights can also be given to animals, the environment, perhaps even robots. Because you have rationality? OK, but what constitutes "rationality"? And do some people, like children, have less rationality than others? Or do you have rights because you are an individual with dignity? Perhaps, but are people only individuals or not also members of relationships and communities? Do they not belong to larger structures of power?

These are difficult questions to answer for the simple reason that the concept of "rights" does not in fact have a single definition. Rather, it has a deep and varied history that has imagined rights in different and even conflicting ways. And this history continues to evolve today.

Even just as a word, the English "right" comes originally from the Indo-European "*reg*," which means "to make straight." Hence the words "regulate," "*regis*" (Latin for "law"), and "rule." The only person to have any rights for most of human history was the "*rex*" or king, who had a "divine right" to regulate, even if implemented via others. It was not until the European Enlightenment of the seventeenth to nineteenth centuries that people began to conceive of "rights" as somehow belonging to large numbers of people. The concept of "human rights" arguably only gained prominence after World War II in the mid-twentieth century. It is no wonder, then, that it is not easy to understand what it might mean to apply the concept of rights to children.

Today's more systematic ideas of rights have their origins in the Enlightenment, which attempted to universalize the power or right to regulate. What we find, however, is that universalization came with a catch: it was defined in such a way as to explicitly exclude many groups and especially children and youth. Indeed, Enlightenment philosophers argued that human rights could be "universal" only if they carved out a public realm only for adults over age twenty-one. Such a position might seem paradoxical to us today. But it made sense at the time because of the way that "rights" themselves came to be theorized.

Let us try to understand this paradox—this conjoining of universalism and adultism—by taking a look at the views of the three most influential Enlightenment philosophers of rights.

John Locke was a seventeenth-century English philosopher and is generally considered the first person to have developed a theory of rights in a systematic and comprehensive way. Locke believed that only adults should have rights because only adults (indeed, really only landowning gentlemen) have a sufficiently developed capacity for "rationality" or "reason" that is necessary to exercise rights.

By Locke's account, it is not just the king who has the right to rule, because it is not just the king who knows what is in the people's best interests. Rather, all rational persons are endowed by their maker with the capacity to know what is best for their own lives. Locke calls this humanity's "natural right" to advance its own "self-preservation," the right to regulate (as in *reg*) one's own life.[3] Specifically, what rational individuals should have the right to regulate is their "property," meaning their life, liberty, and estate (belongings). These are the basic necessities or "rights" for individuals to preserve and advance themselves in the world.

It was using Locke's ideas that the United States Declaration of Independence, for example, states that, instead of being ruled by kings, "all men are created equal, that they are endowed by their Creator with certain unalienable rights, [and] that among these are life, liberty, and the pursuit of happiness." It is no accident that the expression here refers only to "men." The reason why children (not to mention women, minorities, the poor, and slaves) have to be denied these rights is that they lack sufficient rationality to regulate their affairs for themselves.

Here we find Locke's equally influential writings on children. According to Locke, humans do not start out life with full capacities for reason but rather are each a "white page" or *tabula rasa* needing understanding gradually written upon them by others over time.[4] It takes many years for young people's direct sensory experiences of the world to develop into abstract rational competencies. As a result, children are the first and most obvious group of people not to be capable of holding rights. Rather than regulating their own "property," they should remain what Locke calls the "temporary property" of their parents until they gain the competence, around the age of twenty-one, to act rationally in their own self-interest.

Indeed, according to Locke, if children and youth had rights, they would defeat their own self-preservation and do themselves and others harm. The same argument has been used against the rights of many other groups. But it is still used against children today. In the case of Costin, for example, one could use Locke to argue that she lacks sufficient rationality for the right to make her own health decisions. She needs to have those rights exercised on her behalf by competent parents and doctors. The idea that she may herself be capable of rational input is invisible to Lockean theory.

Second, the mid-eighteenth-century French social theorist Jean-Jacques Rousseau excludes children from all rights for a different reason, and one also still influential today. For Rousseau, children do in fact have an innate rationality, installed within them by their creator. But they need it to be protected and nurtured within the private sphere of the home until they are strong and mature enough to use it in a corrupted public world. Children as children are too easily manipulated by the greedy and irrational influences of politics and economics.

A "right" for Rousseau is defined as a freedom to participate in creating one's society's "general will," that is, its shared purposes and structures.[5] Against the natural tendency of societies to fall under the tyranny of a powerful few, rights regimes should create a "social contract" under which societies are ruled by the many. For example, Rousseau's ideas underlay the egalitarian and fraternal ideals of the French Revolution, as in the first article of its Declaration of the Rights of Man and of the Citizen: "Men are born and remain free and equal in rights. Social distinctions may be founded only upon the general good."

Rousseau too wrote a great deal about children. But he argues that children should not be rights-holding citizens, not because they are too irrational, but because they are too weak and innocent. They lack the worldly experience needed to participate in public rights without being corrupted by power and influence. As Rousseau puts it in his book on children's education, *Emile*, children and youth are "noble savages" who need to be sheltered within the private sanctity of the home until such a time as they have sufficiently strengthened their own inner natural and God-given goodness.[6] Indeed, a good and just society depends on the separate nurturance of children in the home so that societal life may continually be infused with new generations of just and independent citizens.

Rousseau would say that Costin, for example, should not have rights to participate in her own health care because she needs to be protected from the various competing influences at play. She deserves to remain in a state of childhood innocence. Instead, the parents, the hospital, and the state should establish general policies for health-care rights that express common public opinion.

Third and finally, the late-eighteenth-century German philosopher Immanuel Kant explicitly excludes children from rights for still another reason. In his view, children lack the requisite "autonomy" or self-rule to exercise rights for themselves. In a somewhat different way than in Locke or Rousseau, Kant argues that humans have rights because, unlike animals, they possess an inherent "dignity" as rational individuals. They are not just means for satisfying each other's desires but also independent, self-ruling ends in themselves.[7] For Kant, human beings are partly like animals, driven by natural instincts and needs, but also partly rational, that is, capable of transcending nature by acting according to higher moral laws. Rights and laws exist in order to impose universal principles and duties upon what would otherwise be a violent conflict of competing wants.

Kant too writes extensively on childhood. The reason Kant denies rights to children is that he views children as not just blank or innocent but as positively irrational. That is, children and youth are chiefly ruled by their own immediate impulses, needs, wants, and desires.[8] They gain the capacity for reason only gradually over time as they learn to discipline their own immediate wants under generalizable moral principles.

As a result, if children had rights, they would not simply lack the competence to exercise them but, worse, use them to advance their own desires regardless of justice to themselves or others. Like in William Golding's novel *Lord of the Flies*, children left to their own devices would quickly turn violent and savage. Interestingly, Kant does in fact allow that children have limited rights *not* to be done violence by others.[9] However, children cannot, in his view, be considered human rights subjects or citizens. They lack the autonomous self-discipline to use public power justly or responsibly. Costin, then, according to Kant, while having a right not to be harmed by others, does not have any other rights because she is incapable of acting fairly or justly herself.

These are the foundations of today's understandings of rights. It is clear why, therefore, we may have difficulty understanding what it might mean for rights to belong specifically to children. The architects of modern rights theory built an edifice of rights meant only to house adults. Indeed, it was constructed to keep children out. It is good that this building is no longer just for the king. But it clearly requires significant renovation if it is to also welcome children.

Specifically, the idea has to be overcome that rights exist to help humanity overcome its initial childlikeness. That rights exist to defeat humanity's irrationality, whether in the form of incompetence, weakness, or unruliness. That rights define a sphere of "adulthood." New theories of rights are needed that either expand these historical foundations or reconstruct them in new ways altogether.

ARE HUMAN RIGHTS TRULY UNIVERSAL?

Let us take a different and equally contentious example: children's rights to work. For here we run headlong into the problem of whether rights are truly universal—adults generally having rights *to* work and children rights *not* to work.

There are at least three competing views on children's rights to work. Some argue that children should have such rights if they are necessary for their or their family's economic survival. For example, MANTHOC, a well-known Latin American child labor union, argues that child and youth work is culturally important and often economically necessary. Others, in contrast, claim that children deserve a right *not* to work, since working necessarily interferes with more important rights, such as to an education and play. For example, in India the Campaign Against Child Labor (CACL) fights against any paid child work because so many Indian children work in exploitative conditions and do not attend school. And others still, such as the International Labour Organization (ILO), take a middle position that children should have certain minimum rights to work but starting at minimum ages and only under conditions that avoid exploitation and harm.[10] The ILO estimates that approximately 211 million children worldwide (or 18 percent of all children) aged five to fourteen are currently employed for wages and that these children deserve both workplace protections and help attending school.[11] (We will explore child labor rights more fully in chapter 5.)

These competing ideas about children's rights to work reflect new developments in human rights theory throughout the twentieth century. These developments both built upon the Enlightenment and revised it in important ways. Most of all, rights theorists wanted to respond to the gross violations of human rights that occurred during World Wars I and II, the Holocaust, and various forms of totalitarianism. They also used ideas from powerful new civil rights movements for racial minorities, colonized peoples, and women.

The central question for the twentieth century became whether human rights could be understood as truly universal. Although in a sense the Enlightenment sought universality, it became clear that many diverse groups had been excluded. What is more, the concept of "the universal" itself had to be rethought since it had so often been used as a cover to impose supposedly "rational" or "civilized" regimes on non-Europeans, women, and racial and ethnic minorities.

The question for us is whether, and to what extent, this new drive for universalism extended, or can be extended, toward children. The answer is that, at least in rights theories, it did not extend toward children in a particularly explicit or extensive way.

Indeed, children almost completely disappear from the discussion. This is better than being explicitly excluded, but only up to a point. At the same time, however, twentieth-century human rights theories at least opened up new options under which children could perhaps be included more fully. The ambiguous upshot is that children do begin to gain different kinds of footing in rights theory, but their specific nature as children receives relatively little attention. Human rights theory goes halfway, as it were, toward taking children seriously.

The first new theory of rights consists of a revision of Kant's ideas, starting in the 1950s in the Anglo-American world, into what came to be known as "will theory." Will theory is still today the dominant view of rights in North American scholarship and society at large. It argues that a human right is most fundamentally of all a protection of the individual will, that is, of individual freedoms, liberties, and autonomy. In this view, all legal, social, and moral rights are ultimately expressions of a single right, as the theorist H. L. A. Hart puts it, "the equal right of all men to be free."[12] The most influential proponent of this view is John Rawls, who describes the basis of social justice as follows: "Each person is to have an equal right to the most extensive scheme of equal basic liberties compatible with a similar scheme of liberties for others."[13] In short, everyone should have the basic right to live according to his or her own individual interests, so long as these interests do not violate this same right for anyone else.

Will theorists such as Rawls generally assume that we are only talking about adults. Nevertheless, their concept of rights has also been applied to children, though with mixed results.

On the positive side, will theory has two benefits for children. First, as in Kant, it insists that no one should use freedoms in a way that violates the freedoms or interests of others. This means that no one has the right, in pursuing his or her own desires, to do children harm or violence. For example, if you employ children in labor, you cannot coerce or exploit them, as in the position of the ILO. And second, perhaps children should after all have at least some freedoms in society. Children may have rights so long as this does not cause harm either to others or to themselves. Freedom no longer depends, as it did for Kant, on possessing supposedly rational autonomy. Rather, freedom is only limited by the extent that it causes harm to others. For example, children may be able to have some rights to free speech, even if not as many such rights as adults, as long as children can use them nondestructively.

On the negative side, however, will theory can easily keep children and youth as second-class citizens. Just as in the Enlightenment, it can be used to deny human rights to those deemed insufficiently competent or independent to exercise their freedoms responsibly. In US law, for example, persons under fourteen are barred from the freedom to pursue paid labor outside the home because it is assumed that they would harm their own childhoods and be subject to exploitation. For the same reasons, children's rights to free speech are easily restricted by schools, courtrooms, and the media. Will theory remains tied to an Enlightenment idea that you only have rights insofar as you are deemed a rationally competent individual.

A second way to theorize human rights today is known as "interest theory." Interest theory is based more on the ideas of Locke and was first developed in the 1970s in Australia and Europe.

Interest theory proposes what could be called a "humanitarian" view, in which human rights exist not simply to protect individual freedoms but more broadly to advance overall human flourishing. People deserve to be provided with rights to "basic forms of human good."[14] All humans should have rights, for example, to life, health care, education, cultural expression, public media, social security, and the like. As in Locke, interest theory protects the right to pursue individual self-interest, but unlike in

Locke, it places an obligation on societies to help provide for those interests as well. A major proponent of interest theory today is Martha Nussbaum, who argues that rights support and advance people's "functional capabilities" to lead fulfilling lives. Everyone should have rights, for example, to bodily health, freedom of thought, affiliation with others, and political participation.[15]

Interest theory arguably stands a better chance than will theory of explaining what it might mean for rights to belong to children. Children and youth obviously need societies to provide them with basic levels of support for their interests. The idea of advancing children's "best interests" is central to the Convention on the Rights of the Child. It may even be the case that young people need interest rights more than do adults, such as to bodily health, education, social affiliation, and economic well-being. Here, the right to work could perhaps be justified for children in cases where their chief interest is basic survival but denied where other interests take precedence such as health or education. Children's work would be a right only insofar as it advanced children's best interests.

The drawback to interest theory, however, when it comes to children, is that it still leaves it mainly up to adults to decide which interests count as rights. This is a problem of power. On the whole, different groups in societies tend to have different degrees of economic, cultural, and political power to determine which interests will be given the greatest consideration. Children as a group almost always have less power than adults. This is why children worldwide are usually the poorest social sector with the least access to health care. Interest theory tends to assume that children do not need to express what their interests actually are, with the result that children's particular and different interests can potentially get lost or ignored.

It is precisely in response to questions of power that a third framework arose for human rights that could be called "liberation theory." Liberation theory was developed in the mid-twentieth century by social reformers such as Mohandas Gandhi, Dorothy Day, and Gustavo Gutiérrez. It animated a wide range of civil rights movements around the world for historically oppressed groups such as the colonized, women, and racial and sexual minorities. It is in a broad sense a radicalization of Rousseau. It seeks to disperse power as broadly as possible, but now recognizing that common democratic rule requires not only equality but also overcoming historical exclusion.

Liberation theory is arguably even more helpful than interest theory when it comes to understanding the rights of children. It helps to inform the worldwide childhood studies movement, which seeks to understand and empower children's own social agency and voice. Children are clearly one of history's most oppressed minorities. It therefore makes sense that they are owed rights to transform their social and political conditions. Only when children have grassroots power of their own are they likely to see genuine and lasting improvements in their collective lives. For example, children's labor rights might be viewed as rights to decide for oneself the extent to which one needs to participate in the labor economy, including the right to fight for inclusion that is nonexploitative. Or children's free speech rights might be understood as ways to empower children to change their worlds.

But liberation theory also has its potential drawbacks. Unlike oppressed adults, it is less clear how children, and especially the youngest of children, should be expected to fight for their rights for themselves. The civil rights model assumes that the oppressed group in question can mobilize and organize itself. While children certainly can, it is also the case that the younger the child, the more the fight for inclusion may depend also on others. Could babies, for example, join together in a movement for adequate day care? At the same time, the truth is that even adults do not simply liberate themselves but also depend on networks of power

to support them. Children expose this potential lacuna in liberation rights theory especially clearly.

Overall, twentieth-century rights theories open up greater possibilities for the inclusion of children than were found in the
Enlightenment. But they have also largely failed to consider the
situation of children in full and explicit ways and so still tend to
assume primacy for adults. They are steps in the right direction,
but there is much further to go. Whether rights are freedoms,
interests, or powers, they can remain ambiguous for children.
They still view children through the lens of adulthood without
responding to the particular experiences of children as children.

WHAT ABOUT CULTURAL RELATIVISM?

A final issue that confronts theories of children's rights is one that
confronts all theories of rights—namely, cultural relativism.

Take, for example, child marriage. In some cultures it is common for girls in particular to marry soon after reaching puberty,
that is, starting at around eleven years old. They typically marry
much older men who have the means to support a wife and family. However, in most cultures today, sex with a minor is considered child abuse, that is, pedophilia, a major violation of children's rights. How much should cultural differences define children's rights? Are children's rights really globally universal, or do
they differ among the world's many social, religious, and ethnic
cultures?

This conundrum is even built into the Convention on the
Rights of the Child. On the one hand, article 30 provides a child
the right "to enjoy his or her own culture." On the other, article
34 guarantees protection "from all forms of sexual exploitation
and sexual abuse." The devil lies in the details. Is girl marriage an
enjoyment of one's own culture or an instance of sexual exploitation? Is the same act of sex with an eleven-year-old abusive in one

community and not in another? And on what basis would one be able to decide?

One aspect of this problem is that "rights" are understood, in all the major twentieth-century theories we have examined, as advancing universal standards. The human rights movement tries to bring everyone into a shared human rights community. It tries to create common policies and norms that treat all persons equally. If indeed it turns out that cultures are completely diverse, then it becomes difficult to see in exactly what sense one may speak any more of "human rights," except perhaps as expressions of a particular set of Western historical values.

Another aspect of the problem is rights' practical "translation" into particular cultural contexts. For example, in Bangalore, India, the government has attempted to promote universal education by banning all children under fourteen from labor. But this move has been opposed by the local child workers union, the Bhima Sangha, that demands instead all children's right to work in order to afford school fees and contribute to family income. Within some local cultures, children's right to work and their right to an education are not opposed. But in other contexts, supposedly universal human rights do not translate into local circumstances.[16]

Finally, there is the broader problem of postcolonialism. It happens that the idea of "universal rights" originated in a time and place—eighteenth-century Europe—that was in the process of colonizing much of the rest of the world. The Global South has seen "universal rights" used to justify overtaking and exploiting groups that were deemed undeveloped or uncivilized by outside powers. None of this is to say that postcolonial societies today cannot usefully employ concepts of rights. All clearly do. But it means that the concept of rights, and perhaps especially children's rights, has itself to be contested in order to uncover hidden justifications for oppression.[17]

Responses to these problems of cultural relativism come in different varieties.

Most of the theorists above—especially will theorists and interest theorists—claim that "human rights" remain universal on some level. They may have to be adjusted for and translated into different cultural contexts. But the problem is one of implementation, not the basic rights themselves. Nussbaum, for example, believes that rights advance a set of basic human capabilities that are shared by all. When confronted with cultural relativism, she argues that "universal norms are actually required if we are to protect diversity, pluralism, and freedom, treating each human being as an agent and an end."[18]

Child marriage, in this view, would most likely be viewed as a fairly basic violation of girls' rights to make their own sexual and life decisions. It may be called for by their larger cultures, but it does not guarantee people who have only just reached sexual maturity a great deal of freedom or agency. It does not advance a girl's basic capabilities to function on her own terms in the world. On the contrary, it keeps girls in a subordinate social position.

Another kind of response, provided by the postmodern theorist Seyla Benhabib, is that cultural differences constantly challenge and transform the very meanings of rights themselves. Human rights do not represent a universal set of values to be translated into particular cultures. On the contrary, they are particular cultural expressions that redefine what it means to have rights in the first place. Benhabib calls these culture-specific interpretations of rights "iterations." That is, rights never stand for original truths but always only culturally appropriated interpretations. "Every iteration transforms meaning, adds to it, enriches it in ever-so-subtle ways. In fact, there is no 'originary' source of meaning, or an 'original' to which all subsequent forms must conform."[19]

From this perspective, child marriage would be something whose rights would need to be debated and interpreted within each particular cultural context. Most of the world might view the key rights here as those needed to protect children and youth from sexual exploitation. However, this idea cannot be assumed to represent an original universal ideal but rather needs to be tested in relation to local understandings. At the same time, child marriage is not simply to be condoned as an expression of cultural history. Rather, the fact that other cultures oppose it means that those in which it is practiced need to justify it carefully. Rights may not be universal norms, but they should spur cultural debate and conversation.

A third kind of response to cultural relativism is to say that rights are means precisely for asserting culturally suppressed voices. Rights can empower persons and groups who fall outside of dominant global power structures. For example, Arjun Appadurai describes the ways in which poor and marginalized groups in the slums of India use the language of rights to organize among themselves and with other such groups around the world. He calls this "grassroots globalization." Local cultures claim the right to fight against the greater powers of colonialism and global neoliberal markets. Rights can be used to promote "those ways of thinking, feeling, and acting that increase the horizons of hope, that expand the field of the imagination, . . . and that widen the field of informed, creative, and critical citizenship."[20]

Child marriage in this view would be complex. On the one hand, girls and local communities might be encouraged to organize, among themselves and with other such local communities, to fight for their grassroots rights to pursue local traditions against the imposition of dominant norms. On the other hand, girls themselves might wish to organize with other girls in the same situation to fight against child marriage if they find it to be oppressive within their own community contexts. Whether child marriage remains a right or not would depend, in this view, on which form of oppression is worse: global or traditional. And so it would depend most crucially of all on what such girls themselves experience. The crucial right is for oppressed groups to become empowered.

CAN CHILDREN BE INCLUDED?

None of these contemporary theoretical perspectives, however, has seriously considered the rights of children. Will theory, interest theory, and liberationism are all focused primarily on adults, as are the various ways of addressing today's global realities of cultural relativism. While eighteenth- and nineteenth-century rights theorists discussed children at length in order to explain why they should be excluded, twentieth- and twenty-first-century rights theorists rarely explicitly take children into account.

Nevertheless, in recent years, several rights theorists have started to explore children's inclusion. These are attempts at what I am calling childism. That is, they go beyond assuming that children can simply be added on under theories based on the rights of adults. Instead, they revise rights theory itself in light of children's particular lives. They try to expand what it means to have rights in the first place, for children and adults both. It is one thing to give children the same rights as adults in a lesser way. It is another to reconceptualize rights altogether so that children are included equally as children.

These attempts in effect challenge the original binary opposition from the Enlightenment between adults and children. The fundamental problem is that rights are based on supposedly "adult" competencies for reason, debate, and independence. As long as such is the case, children will have rights in only second-hand ways. But are adults really so autonomous and independent? And are children really the opposite? Or is it not more accurate to say that no one is fully an island to oneself, just as no one is fully dependent on others? It may be time for this adult-child divide to be overcome.

One way to include children explicitly in rights theory, advanced by the prominent children's rights lawyer Barbara Bennett Woodhouse, is to base rights not on individual autonomy but on relational interdependence. The world is not composed of independent adults and dependent children. Rather, all persons, adult and child, are interdependent. They act and speak for themselves but with the support of diverse networks of social relationship. All humans, regardless of age, express their agency and voice only within the context of families, communities, cultures, and political and legal systems.

As a result, according to Woodhouse, both adults and children deserve both "needs-based rights" based on their dependency on others to provide them with support and "capacity-based rights" based on their ability to express their own agency and voice.[21] The purpose of rights is to maximize human dignity by ensuring the fullest possible combination of both kinds of rights for everyone.

Take again the example of labor rights. The traditional view is that labor rights are rights to work autonomously and without interference. Hence adults deserve them and children do not. From an interdependency view, in contrast, labor rights could be understood as rights to be fully included within shared economic relations. In societies that can afford it, children's rights to work may be superseded by their rights to an education that will permit them greater work opportunities in the future. But in societies threatened by poverty and starvation, children's rights to economic inclusion may instead involve at least partial rights to work, with other rights such as the right to an education being balanced alongside them. It would still be necessary, as asserted by the ILO, for children's labor rights always to include rights to nonexploitation, because exploitation abuses persons' economic interdependency. But the underlying question is not how to preserve economic autonomy but rather how to include all in systems of shared economic interdependency.

Another way to include children in rights theory is to base rights not on rationality but on diversity or difference. The feminist philosopher Ruth Lister, for example, argues that children, like women and men, have the basic right to have society recognize their uniquely different lived experiences. What counts as important in society is too often determined by a powerful few. Instead, in advancing human rights, "our goal should be a universalism which stands in creative tension to diversity and difference and which challenges the divisions and exclusionary inequalities which stem from diversity."[22]

Children, in this view, are owed equal rights because they are just as different and diverse as anyone else. Indeed, children are the most marginalized societal group of all and so the group most in need of rights to recognition of their differences. Children show that rights are not fixed expressions of rationality or power but rather evolving expressions of "lived citizenship" that empower diverse societal groups to engage in "dialectical struggle" with one another.[23]

Lister provides the example of the kind of children's parliaments with which this book began. Children's parliaments, from this perspective, do not simply extend to children the same competence-based rights that are already held by adults. Rather, they reach into children's own particular lives, in their local communities and schools, and open up opportunities for them to influence political agendas using their own distinctive voices and experiences. Children's parliaments include children in political life by opening up societies to children's otherwise ignored political perspectives.

It is also possible, as I attempt in my own work, to combine interdependency and difference. In this view, rights can be understood as "social responsibilities to the human diversity of otherness."[24] Because humans are irreducibly diverse, they depend upon one another for being respected and included in their public worlds. The basic purpose of rights is to render societal networks of interdependency as fully responsive as possible to the differences of experience within them.

An example would be the right to publicly funded education. (We will return to education rights in depth in chapter 4.) In most countries, this right belongs chiefly to children and youth aged around five to seventeen. Some wealthier countries extend versions of this right to young adults in university, while other generally poorer countries guarantee this right only through primary school. To have a "right" to a publicly funded education means that society owes a responsibility to children's distinctive situation of educational need. Children have this right in particular, not because they are in the process of becoming future independent adults, but because, in the here and now as children, they belong to interdependent networks responsible for educational provision. Other groups, such as the elderly or women, stand in need, likewise, of other kinds of interdependent public response, such as social security or maternity leave, according to their own particular experiences and conditions.

Whether the emphasis is placed on interdependence, difference, or responsiveness, human rights theory can be rethought fundamentally to include children. Rights theory is always evolving and how it responds to children will change over time. But the three views described here are all moving in much the same direction. They reject the Enlightenment assumption that rights exist primarily to protect and advance individual autonomy. They also reject the view held throughout the twentieth century that children do not need to factor into theoretical considerations. Rather, children will gain their rights only when rights themselves are understood in broader and more complex ways. Rights in one way or another should include everyone and so be based not on a preconceived adult model but on humanity's full diversity.

CONCLUSION

We find, then, that human rights theory has slowly evolved from explicitly excluding children to ignoring but potentially including children secondarily and finally to recent beginnings at including children centrally and explicitly.

The adultism of human rights theory is profound. It is an expression of ancient patriarchal biases that exclude not only by gender but also by age. These biases will take significant cultural and political struggle to be overcome. It is still predominantly the case today that children are thought too incompetent, weak, or dependent to enjoy human rights as fully as adults. But it is also the case that rights theory is not set in stone and has proved itself able to change over time in response to previously marginalized groups. From this perspective, the major human rights struggle still facing humanity is to find a way to include everyone fully, regardless of age.

In the next chapter, we see how some of these theoretical debates have played out in actual children's rights movements over history. On the whole, human rights theory has lagged behind actual children's rights practices. Theory and practice influence each other. But in the case of children's rights, it has largely fallen to children and child advocates to press for creative new solutions to very real problems. At the same time, children's actual rights remain far from complete, so innovations in rights theory still hold promise for helping to point the way forward.

Children will ultimately fail to gain their due rights insofar as rights continue to be assumed as primarily modeled on adulthood. New ways of theorizing rights will need to be developed to include children fully. The challenge here is to imagine what human rights would really mean if they no longer prioritized one age over another.

3

HISTORICAL AMBIGUITIES

Raikan is a fourteen-year-old girl who spends her days working alongside several dozen other children and youth aged ten to seventeen in the tobacco fields of Kazakhstan. She has spent the last two years performing nine to eighteen hours a day of physically demanding labor for five to seven days a week. She is one of an estimated 5.5 million children around the world working in slave-like conditions today.[1]

Raikan has blisters on her face and neck from sunburn, is exposed to unregulated pesticides and fertilizers, and is occasionally injured by the sharp tools she uses to cut the plants. She risks acute nicotine poisoning through her fingers from handling the tobacco leaves and has not been to school since she arrived. Her work produces inexpensive tobacco for Philip Morris International, the US company that makes several of the fifteen top cigarette brands in the world, including the world's leading brand, Marlboro.

Raikan's situation illustrates a profound historical ambiguity.

On the one hand, children now enjoy such a tremendous array of rights that the continued existence of something like child slavery appears to most of us profoundly shocking.

The young had virtually no rights at all until about two hundred years ago. But now there is a global consensus that the rights of children and youth are many. Protection against exploitative labor stands at the top of the list, a list that also includes rights against violence and discrimination and rights to schooling, health care, free speech, and much else. Indeed, it was to fight situations like Raikan's that the children's rights movement first began in the factories and slums of Europe in the early nineteenth century. Raikan's work also violates almost a century of international law against child-labor exploitation, starting with the International Labour Organization's (ILO's) 1930 Forced Labour Convention and going all the way up through the United Nations' 1989 Convention on the Rights of the Child (CRC) and the ILO's 1999 Worst Forms of Child Labour Convention. And it runs afoul of Kazakhstani laws against minors working under long, unsafe, and dangerous conditions and being trafficked, kept out of school, and denied freedom of movement.

On the other hand, children in every corner of the world remain very much second-class rights citizens.

Child exploitation remains widespread in part because children's rights often take a backseat to those of adults. Child slavery, as we will see in chapter 5, has, if anything, grown in recent decades due to the globalization of markets and the declining power of nations to regulate them. More broadly, children gained their rights much later in history than adults and often only in partial and borrowed ways. Even the very idea of children's rights, as we saw in the previous chapter, remains for some in dispute.

This chapter examines why children's rights remain so ambiguous and even paradoxical today by unearthing some of their complex historical roots over the past two centuries. How did the children's rights movement first come about? How did it overcome theoretical resistance to the idea of children having rights at all? What have been its major goals and achievements? In what ways has it shifted emphasis over time? Why did it become increasingly international? And how effective has it been in improving the real lives of children?

For the sake of simplicity, the children's rights movement can be said to have developed in three phases or waves, each adding a new element to those before. I describe these phases as a movement from "child saving" to "child protection" to "child empowerment." The nineteenth-century children's rights movement tended to focus on saving children's childhoods; the twentieth-century, on protecting children from violence and abuse; and now the twenty-first, on empowering children to act on their own behalf. These movements have not replaced each other so much as built upon one another like waves on a shore.

DO CHILDREN HAVE RIGHTS TO BE SAVED?

What I am calling the first wave of children's rights began in Europe in the early to middle nineteenth century. Of course, children had previously had "rights" in a general moral sense, such as not to be murdered or done violence to, though these were almost always under the jurisdiction of families rather than nations. What was new in the nineteenth century was a growing concern about whether and to what extent the public realm should step in and provide children with rights to be saved from exploited and miserable lives.

The children's rights movement did not grow, as the modern adults' rights movement had before it, out of Enlightenment democratization. (Indeed, the children's rights movement follows almost exactly the opposite path from the adults' rights movement, since the latter began in democratic empowerment rights and only in the last century extended into adults' rights to societal provisions like welfare and health care.) Rather, the children's rights movement grew out of the perceived dangers to children of the new and rapid rise of industrialization. In response, a growing number of charities, organizations, and governments came to embrace the fight to save children from factory exploitation and growing urban poverty. They sought to provide what the American author and reformer Kate Douglas Wiggin famously called "the right to a childhood."[2]

Industrialization created a sharper division than had existed before in history between people's private and public spheres of life. Beforehand, men, women, and children typically lived and worked alongside one another on the farm or in the family business, which combined private and public life as one. When work increasingly moved outside the home into factories, it created the possibility that children and youth would find themselves spending long days outside the home and in exploitative conditions. Factory owners found in children cheap and malleable sources of labor. What is more, industrialization created vast impoverished urban slums in which children found themselves without traditional economic community supports and with less healthy living conditions. And at the same time, industrialization demanded increasing levels of education to which many children lacked access.

A growing number of public intellectuals and social reformers began to make the argument that industrial life was denying large numbers of children the right to a childhood. What they meant is that long hours in factories and poverty in slums prevented children from growing up in supportive and nurturing environments. This view represents a kind of Rousseauean romanticism. Children need to grow up outside of artificial public life within the more natural private sphere of home and family. But unlike in Rousseau himself, and because of industrialization, children's private lives now came to be seen as needing active promotion not just by parents but also by public government rights.

It is no accident that the first stirrings of children's legal rights took place in the United Kingdom, the country in which the Industrial Revolution began. Perhaps the earliest substantive children's rights document in history is the Factory Act of 1802. In it, the UK parliament provided factory apprentices, who were as young as five, the rights to a clean and ventilated work environment, a small amount of daily education, monthly religious services, and a workday not to last more than twelve hours.

Although this act was never effectively implemented, it did lay the groundwork for a series of increasingly enforceable acts that culminated in the UK's Factory Act of 1833. Here, children under nine were banned from factory labor altogether, those nine to thirteen limited to forty-eight hours a week, and those fourteen to seventeen limited to sixty-nine hours a week. In addition, children in factories had to be provided at least two hours of schooling a day. And, most important, the government appointed "factory inspectors" to ensure the act's effective implementation. Further UK bills in 1842 and 1847 guaranteed children's rights, respectively, to a minimum working age of ten and to not working more than ten hours a day.[3]

Similar legal rights for child laborers were subsequently adopted throughout the nineteenth century in Europe, North America, and other parts of the world. For example, India passed the Factories Act of 1881, setting a minimum age of child wage labor of seven and a maximum of nine hours a day with at least four holidays a month.[4]

Toward the end of the nineteenth century, this notion of saving children's childhood began to expand to include other kinds of rights as well. Children started to gain rights, for example, to a basic education, orphanages in the absence of parents, and a separate juvenile justice system. In one way or another, adults sought to make sure that children were provided rights to their own separate sphere of childhood.

In terms of education, by 1870 all states in the United States, a leader in this area, had established the right to a free and universal elementary school education. In 1872, Japan created its first national system of universal children's education called the "Fundamental Code of Education."[5] In 1877, the New Zealand Parliament made it compulsory for children to attend school up to the age of fourteen. In 1882, the Jules Ferry laws in France created the first national system of universal, compulsory, free, gender-equal, and secular education, guaranteeing all children government-funded full-time schooling up to the age of fifteen. And in 1893 the first states in India began to guarantee the right to a compulsory elementary education.[6]

This same period saw Europe and North America institute the first juvenile justice systems, intended to protect children from the adult justice system and provide distinct criminal procedures focused on rehabilitation rather than punishment. These reformers saw themselves as "child savers" marking out special services that would prevent children from falling into adult courts and prisons.[7] Along similar lines, in 1889 the United Kingdom established the National Society for the Prevention of Cruelty to Children, aimed at fostering legal and social rights against child abuse and neglect. One of its founders, Benjamin Waugh, famously asserted that "the rights of a child are its birthrights," meaning that children are owed rights to their own childhoods.[8]

This first wave of the children's rights movement arguably reached its peak in the League of Nations' landmark 1924 Declaration of the Rights of the Child. This declaration (also known as the Geneva Declaration) was the first truly international human rights agreement in all of history. It was drafted by the British social reformer Eglantyne Jebb, who in 1919 had founded Save the Children, still a preeminent global non-governmental children's rights organization. Jebb was initially motivated by efforts to alleviate children's starvation in Germany and Austria-Hungary during the Allied blockade of World War I. But the resulting 1924 declaration broadened the scope to fight children's extreme suffering worldwide.

The 1924 declaration is what today would be called a primarily "provision" rights document. This means that its major aim was to actively provide children with the basic necessities for survival and development. As the preface puts it, "mankind owes to the Child the best that it has to give." Specifically, children should have rights to the means for normal development (article 1); food, health care, rehabilitation, and shelter (article 2); relief in times of distress (article 3); a basic level of training or education (article 4); and a sense of devotion to the service of fellow men (article 5). Governments and organizations are called upon to invest sufficient public resources to provide children a healthy and thriving childhood.

Even if these rights remain limited by today's standards, and even if they only touched the lives of a minority of children worldwide, it is still true to say that they represented a revolution in the history of human rights. Over a period of only about a century, the children's rights movement grew from nothing into a broadly supported international campaign. This growth far exceeds the children's rights theory discussed in the previous chapter, which, as we saw, did not start taking children's rights seriously until well into the late twentieth century. It was practical efforts to improve the lives of real children that led the way.

At the same time, as we can now see in hindsight, this first wave of children's rights remains ambiguous. The rights it provides to children are designed precisely to keep children sequestered in their own private sphere. It does not imagine children to be members of the public rights community. In other words, it does not treat children as human rights subjects, capable of fighting for rights themselves, but only as objects of paternalistic concern from adults. This approach compares to the way that women had also been treated, even though it is exactly around this time, throughout the nineteenth century, that women started to move in the opposite direction to demand public rights to participation in work, civil society, and politics.

The paradox, then, in this first wave of the children's rights movement, is that children started to gain public rights only insofar as those rights separated children into their own private sphere of home and school. This is not to say that children did not—and do not still—need to be provided these kinds of special rights. But it does mean that children's rights "saved" children only by removing them from public life. Industrialization created separate public and private spheres for adults, but increasingly only a private sphere for children. This kind of separation may empower children as future adults but tends to disempower children as children.

DO CHILDREN HAVE SPECIAL RIGHTS TO PROTECTION?

The problem with child saving came to a head with World War II. Here it became all too depressingly obvious that childhood could not be separated into a safe, private bubble. During the 1939–1945 war across Europe and East Asia, children were equally if not disproportionately the victims of advanced technological violence and genocide. They were killed and maimed by aerial bombings of cities, mass warfare across the countryside, the use of atom bombs on civilians, and the genocide of the Holocaust. They were at least as likely as adults to suffer from ethnic cleansing, colonial aggression, and totalitarian oppression.

The years after World War II ushered in a rebirth of the human rights movement as the best way to say "never again" to humanity's tremendous capacities for inhumanity. The world awoke to societies' abilities to systematically trample human dignity. The United Nations was founded accordingly in 1945 "to save succeeding generations from the scourge of war . . . [and] to reaffirm faith in fundamental human rights, in the dignity and worth of the human person, in the equal rights of men and women and of nations large and small."[9] Likewise, as we saw in the previous chapter, scholars worked to develop new and more thoroughly universal human rights theories. And it was in the wake of World War II that there began an explosion of civil rights movements, such as those against colonial rule in India, male patriarchy in the workplace, and racial segregation in the United States, all fighting against system-wide societal injustices.

What did this mean for the rights of children? The children's rights movement did not abandon its previous child-saving efforts. But it developed into a new wave that began to emphasize instead children's needs for special societal protections. To provision rights was added a new category of protection rights—rights, that is, to children's protection against the active violence and abuse that comes from generally more powerful adults and societies. Children are now to be both saved *by* adults and protected *from* them.

This shift in emphasis can be described as a shift from positive rights to negative rights: from children's provision rights *for* a flourishing childhood to children's protection rights *against* violence and harm from others. Indeed, without negative protections such as against abuse and discrimination, positive rights such as to health and education cannot be realized. Raikan can go to school only if she is protected against long hours or labor exploitation.

In theoretical terms, we see a shift here from Rousseauean rights to flourishing to Kantian rights against violations of basic human dignity. Unlike for Kant himself, however, now these violations are not understood as simply undermining adult rational autonomy. Indeed, rationality itself became suspect after the supposedly "rational" projects of the Nazi ideal of a pure race, the

Stalinist and Maoist purges of nonconformists, and colonialism's drives to "civilize" the world. The door opened to include children as being owed dignity and respect, not based on a shared human autonomy, but based on a shared human vulnerability to harm from others.

Concretely speaking, this new drive to give children protection rights first appears internationally in the United Nations' 1948 Universal Declaration of Human Rights. This declaration, the landmark human rights document of the twentieth century, only mentions children specifically twice, and each time only in passing (in subclauses of articles 25 and 26). But, as the title "universal" suggests, all articles but one (article 16, on the right to marriage) speak in terms of the rights not just of "adults" but of "everyone" and "all."

Thus, for example, the 1948 declaration insists that everyone is "born free and equal in dignity and rights" (article 1) and "without distinction of any kind" (2). All are accordingly owed rights such as to "life, liberty and security of person" (3), "equal protection of the law" (7), "privacy" (12), "freedom of movement" (13), "freedom of thought, conscience, and religion" (18), and "education" (26). However, children are probably not meant to be included in "universal and equal suffrage" (21) and "free choice of employment" (23).

Children's rights in particular are addressed through the UN's creation in 1946 of the United Nations Children's Fund (UNICEF). In a similar way to Save the Children, UNICEF was initially formed to provide European children with emergency food and health care after the devastation of World War II. But it quickly took on a broader mandate, especially after it was due to expire in 1950. This mandate included not only providing for impoverished children but also protecting children worldwide against all manner of violence and abuse. UNICEF has now worked for decades, and continues to be the world's leading organization, in not only providing children means for survival, health, and basic education, but also protecting children against gender and disability discrimination, war and civil violence, and sexual and labor exploitation.

This new wave of the children's rights movement fully gathered momentum with the UN's drafting of the 1959 Declaration of the Rights of the Child. This declaration expands the earlier 1924 declaration above. It lists ten basic children's rights: four of the same kind of provision rights as in 1924, but six representing the new kind of protection rights. These protection rights are against "discrimination on account of race, colour, sex, language, religion," and so on (principle 1); "special protection . . . [of] the best interests of the child" (2); "a name and a nationality" (3); priority of children in "protection and relief" (8); against "all forms of neglect, cruelty and exploitation" (9); and against "racial, religious and any other form of discrimination" (10).

Protection rights now come first and last on the list and constitute the majority of rights overall. Children need to be protected from harm if they are also to be provided healthy and thriving lives.

This shift in emphasis can also be seen at the national level. For instance, in the United States, perhaps the most important children's rights advance in the twentieth century was the Supreme Court's 1954 decision in *Brown v. Board of Education*. Up to this point, all children in the United States already enjoyed the provision right to an education. What the *Brown* decision acknowledged is that the provision of children's education cannot succeed in reality without the additional protection of children against educational discrimination. The Supreme Court decided that deep racial disparities across society meant that "separate educational facilities [for black and white children] are inherently unequal." Educational achievement depends on educational nondiscrimination.

Similar shifts in US law would soon follow for other systematically violated groups of children. For example, the 1967 Supreme
Court decision *In re Gault* gave juvenile delinquents due process
protections in court. Title IX of the US Education Amendments
of 1972 prohibited discrimination in school activities based on
sex. The 1974 Child Abuse Prevention and Treatment Act for the
first time created meaningful and effective legislation to combat
child abuse, injecting public protection rights for children into
the private realm of the home.

The twentieth century also saw an explosion in the growth of
non-governmental organizations (NGOs) dealing with children's
rights to protection. There are hundreds of NGOs for children
worldwide, some international and others local. For example, an
NGO in Thailand called the Development and Education Programme for Daughters and Communities (DEPDC) has fought
since 1988 for girls' protections against being sold into prostitution. In the United States, the Children's Defense Fund, founded
in 1973 by the civil rights attorney Marian Wright Edelman, has
fought for children's provision and protection rights in areas as
diverse as welfare reform, racial discrimination, juvenile justice,
education policy, health-care coverage, disability, adoption, and
foster care. Providing children with flourishing lives is deeply
intertwined with protecting children from systemic discrimination.

The most powerful expression of this child protection wave
may have been the 1990 World Summit for Children, held at the
United Nations headquarters in New York City and involving the
then largest gathering ever of heads of state in history. A total of
159 countries pledged under a jointly signed "World Declaration
on the Survival, Protection and Development of Children" to advance twenty-seven children's rights goals over the course of the
decade to come. Leaders pledged "to give every child a better
future," since "the children of the world are innocent, vulnerable

and dependent." According to the UN, these efforts have achieved some successes, such as the eradication of polio and guinea worm disease and a reduction in under-five child mortality; but they have also fallen short in areas such as rights to a primary education, routine immunizations, and labor nonexploitation.

One could also point along similar lines to the UN's Millennium Development Goals (MDGs) of 2000, which, while not focused solely on children, do include many children's rights concerns. The MDGs declare "a collective responsibility to uphold the principles of human dignity, equality and equity at the global level . . . [including] a duty therefore to all the world's people, especially the most vulnerable and, in particular, the children of the world, to whom the future belongs."[10] For children in particular, these goals combine provision rights such as to primary schooling, economic stability, and a sustainable environment, with protection rights such as against under-five mortality, involvement in armed conflict, and genocide.

Overall, this second wave of the children's rights movement reached a consensus that provision and protection rights mutually reinforce each other. Simply providing children a childhood is not enough. Children also need their childhoods protected against adult harm and societal injustice.

Again, however, in retrospect, there still remains much ambiguity and even paradox.

On the one hand, the world clearly committed itself during this period to serious children's rights causes. And children today, as a result, enjoy vastly broader and more systematic rights than ever before. The world now recognizes that children are especially vulnerable to human rights abuses. Children are no longer merely to be secluded in a separate private sphere.

On the other hand, children remain throughout this period and still today very much second-class citizens. They are the poorest age group in all countries, having throughout the twentieth century generally overtaken the elderly in this respect. In the United States, they continue to face racial discrimination in education and the justice system. And they have far fewer rights worldwide to free speech, public assembly, and standing in courts.

Some would argue that this situation is because the children's rights movement is still relatively new and needs more time to succeed. This view is implicit in the 1990 World Declaration and the 2000 Millennium Development Goals, which call for renewed efforts toward children's rights implementation.

But others argue that there remains a problem with how children's rights are understood. Children's rights continue to be framed during this wave as separate from adults' rights. The separation is no longer simply private rights versus public rights, as in the earlier child saving movement. Rather, it is between different kinds of public rights: protection/provision rights for all versus participation/empowerment rights only for adults. That is, children's rights are instruments by which vulnerable and passive children are given special provisions and protections by independent and agentic adults. Children are not imagined as participants in creating and enacting rights themselves.

This situation contrasts sharply with the rights being gained during this time by adults. The many civil rights movements starting in the 1950s sought precisely to empower previously disempowered groups such as women and ethnic, racial, and sexual minorities. But civil rights to self-empowerment were never seriously applied to the most disempowered group of all, children. Rather, the assumption persisted, deeply rooted in history, that the young are simply not capable of their own public agency and voice.

And so in a sense, despite tremendous gains, children's rights during this period continue to function paradoxically as ways of empowering adults and disempowering children, this time in the name of protecting children from adult harm.

DO CHILDREN HAVE RIGHTS TO EMPOWERMENT?

This problem of children's lack of empowerment started to be recognized by academics and advocates in the 1970s and 1980s. As we see from the previous discussions, these early stirrings of a more participatory approach were largely drowned out by focuses on child saving and child protection. Nevertheless, a third wave of children's rights can be identified as beginning to gather momentum toward the end of the twentieth century around the question of whether children and youth should, in the end, also enjoy rights to act, speak freely, and exercise influence in the public sphere.

These rights are generally thought of as a "third P," after provision and protection rights, of participation rights. Participation rights are rights to play an active role in public life.

Let us return again to the example of the slave laborer Raikan. For adults, slave labor has not historically been defeated by provisions and protections alone. It ultimately requires, as for example in the US South, that oppressed groups gain participation kinds of rights to public freedoms and power. In the case of children like Raikan, it is true that greater implementation of antilabor protections will help. But ultimately, such children may need to be empowered to participate in societies on their own behalf. That is, they may deserve to be treated as full human rights subjects.

As we saw in the previous chapter, it is precisely because participation rights are so fundamental to modern conceptions of adulthood that they tend to be denied to children. But it has now become apparent to many in the children's rights community that without some level of public power of their own, children will still remain second-class citizens. Their rights need to guarantee them a more solid foundation of public dignity and respect.

The very earliest stirrings of this third wave of children's rights grew out of the earlier-mentioned civil rights movements for adults. Children's advocates, including children themselves, noticed that while every other group was gaining rights to civic participation, such rights remained largely unthinkable for the most disempowered third of the population of all. Writers such as John Holt and Jonathan Kozol began to argue that the same logic should apply to children. Children would not gain real and lasting rights in any area of society without greater abilities to act and raise their voices in the public realm for themselves.

Such ideas also started to take shape in the nascent "childhood studies" or "new sociology of childhood" movement that began in Britain, Scandinavia, and northern Europe in the early 1980s. This movement sought a new way to study children as not just adults in development but agents with voices in their own right. As described by two of the founders of childhood studies, Allison James and Alan Prout, children need to be understood as "actively involved in the construction of their own social lives, the lives of those around them and of the societies in which they live."[11] Children are not merely passive objects of adult socialization but construct the meanings of their lives, and in multiple ways, for themselves.

This new approach to scholarship about children gave rise to two major consequences for children's rights. First, children's rights could be studied, not only from the perspective of adults, but also from the ground-up perspectives of children themselves. Scholars realized they needed to ask children, in all their social and cultural diversity, about their own experiences and views concerning their rights. And second, the concept that children are social agents places the central emphasis on children's rights to participation. The full implementation of all children's rights depends on children's most basic rights of all to speak and act as citizens in society on their own behalf.

There are now many different ways in which children are gaining rights to participation in the public sphere. We have already witnessed some of them, such as in children's parliaments and labor unions. In subsequent chapters, we will examine several more in the areas of education, economics, and politics.

But here let us focus on the signal achievement in children's participation rights so far, and indeed the signal achievement of the children's rights movement overall: the United Nations' 1989 Convention on the Rights of the Child (CRC). With the CRC, the third wave of children's rights truly starts to gain momentum.

The CRC is one of the most important human rights documents in history. First, it is the most widely ratified human rights treaty ever, including every single country in the world but one. This one exception, for reasons we will discuss later, is the United States, even though the United States was one of the CRC's leading drafters. Second, unlike the 1924 and 1959 declarations, the CRC is a "convention," meaning that its articles are enforceable. The mechanism for enforcement is a UN-appointed Committee on the Rights of the Child that is created for each ratifying nation and empowered to produce a report every five years on that country's children's rights progress. Enforcement is not by legal action but by international exposure of children's rights violations and pressure to redress them. (It is important to note that countries can and generally do make "reservations" when ratifying the CRC. For example, India has a reservation against banning child labor, and Iran has a reservation that nothing shall contravene Islamic law.)

But third and most important, the CRC is a landmark document because for the first time in international law it includes children's rights to public participation. These participation rights are the most controversial of all the rights in the CRC but also the

most groundbreaking and empowering. They are laid out alongside the CRC's other rights to provision and protection. Indeed,
the UN explicitly describes the CRC's rights as falling into the
"three Ps" of provision, protection, and participation. In effect,
children's participation rights completely overturn the original
Enlightenment ideal of rights as a sphere of adult-only participation.

Of the CRC's forty children's rights overall, approximately fifteen (depending on how they are counted) are the same kind of
provision rights as found in the 1924 declaration, though now
greatly expanded. They include one of the core CRC rights to the
advancement of every child's "best interests" (article 3). They also
include, for example, "the right to life" and "maximum . . . survival and development" (article 6); "a name [and] nationality" (7);
assistance from the state if deprived of a family (20); a regulated
"system of adoption" (21); "a full and decent life" for every "mentally or physically disabled child" (23); "the highest attainable
standard of health" (24); "the right to benefit from social security"
(26); "a standard of living adequate for the child's physical, mental, spiritual, moral and social development" (27); free and compulsory primary school education for all (28 and 29); "rest and
leisure," including "cultural, artistic, recreational and leisure ac-
tivity" (31); and measures for child victims' "physical and psychological recovery and social reintegration" (39).

An additional nineteen or so of the CRC's forty rights are the
same kind of protection rights as found in the 1959 declaration,
but again greatly expanded. These include, for example, rights
against "discrimination of any kind," including on the basis of
race, color, sex, and religion (article 2); respect for the "responsibilities, rights and duties" of parents and extended family (5);
noninterference with each child's "identity, including nationality,
name and family relations" (8); that, except when necessary, a
child "not be separated from his or her parents against their will"

(9); against "illicit transfer . . . abroad" (11); against "all forms of physical or mental violence, injury or abuse, neglect or negligent treatment, maltreatment or exploitation, including sexual abuse" (19); refugee children's "appropriate protection and humanitarian assistance" (22); for ethnic minority children to enjoy their own culture, religion, and language (30); "to be protected from economic exploitation" (32); against "all forms of sexual exploitation and sexual abuse" (34); "the abduction of, the sale of or traffic in children" (35); "torture or other cruel, inhuman or degrading treatment or punishment," including capital punishment and life imprisonment (37); for children under fifteen not to take part in armed conflicts (38); and to enjoy the basic protections of "penal law" (40).

No international legal instrument had previously contained, however, a third kind of children's right to active public participation. There are six participation rights in the CRC, and they are worth examining in some detail. The first three set out general principles and the last three means to their implementation.

The most often cited participation right is article 12, which calls upon states to assure children's rights to express their views freely in all judicial, administrative, and other matters concerning them. It reads, in full:

1. States Parties shall assure to the child who is capable of forming his or her own views the right to express those views freely in all matters affecting the child, the views of the child being given due weight in accordance with the age and maturity of the child.
2. For this purpose, the child shall in particular be provided the opportunity to be heard in any judicial and administrative proceedings affecting the child, either directly, or through a representative or an appropriate body, in a manner consistent with the procedural rules of national law.

As we discuss later on, this free expression right is more restrictive than such rights generally are for adults. Nevertheless, a legal guarantee is put in place to empower children to speak up in certain public realms on their own behalf. It would demand, for example, were the United States to ratify the CRC, that minors have the right to speak in judicial proceedings, a right they are not currently guaranteed in most states.

Article 13 broadens children's right to freedom of expression by limiting restrictions on it to similar limitations as usually found for adults, such as respect for others and protection of public order:

1. The child shall have the right to freedom of expression; this right shall include freedom to seek, receive and impart information and ideas of all kinds, regardless of frontiers, either orally, in writing or in print, in the form of art, or through any other media of the child's choice.
2. The exercise of this right may be subject to certain restrictions, but these shall only be such as are provided by law and are necessary: (a) For respect of the rights or reputations of others; or (b) For the protection of national security or of public order, or of public health or morals.

This right appears to target free expression in public media rather than specific judicial and administrative matters. It remains silent on whether it includes educational settings and politics, though arguably it could.

Article 14 extends these freedom rights to matters of thought, conscience, and religion. It states, again in full:

1. States Parties shall respect the right of the child to freedom of thought, conscience and religion.
2. States Parties shall respect the rights and duties of the parents and, when applicable, legal guardians, to provide direction to the child in the exercise of his or her right in a manner consistent with the evolving capacities of the child.

3. Freedom to manifest one's religion or beliefs may be subject only to such limitations as are prescribed by law and are necessary to protect public safety, order, health or morals, or the fundamental rights and freedoms of others.

These freedoms are again somewhat more limited than for adults, out of respect for the rights of parents and children's evolving capacities. Still, they empower children to exercise some degree of freedom of conscience and religion, making this a controversial right for some.

Finally, articles 15 to 17 guarantee children various means for exercising their freedoms effectively. Article 15 guarantees "the rights of the child to freedom of association and to freedom of peaceful assembly." This is an important right because it protects children's abilities to enter physically into the public sphere. Article 16 states that "no child shall be subjected to arbitrary or unlawful interference with his or her privacy, family, or correspondence, nor to unlawful attacks on his or her honour and reputation." The reason this may be considered a participation right is that it preserves freedom of thought and expression within the private sphere. And article 17 requires that "States Parties . . . shall ensure that the child has access to information and material from a diversity of national and international sources." Children can participate in society in a meaningful way only if they are guaranteed a degree of free access to information and mass media.

These participation rights may be few and limited, but they have become a rallying call for children and children's advocates worldwide. They were in part the inspiration behind the rise of children's parliaments and children's labor unions in the 1990s. They support children who are championing their own rights in schools and communities. They are cited by researchers and scholars who seek to understand and respond to children's own voices on social issues. And, as we will see in the next chapters, they weave their way through all manner of rights concerning education, labor, and politics.

The CRC overall has become the benchmark and rallying call for children's rights worldwide. Its success could be said to lie in its complexity. By combining provision, protection, and participation rights in the same document, it puts children on the human rights agenda as fully rounded human beings. It goes beyond simple child saving and even just children's special protection. For it seeks in part also to treat children as legitimate public participants in their own right. The public arena of rights is no longer a one-way street that adults apply to children but a two-way street in which children also participate in impacting public rights for themselves.

The story of the CRC has only just begun. It has been amended already with three "optional protocols" (OPs) in which aspects of the CRC are further expanded upon. So far, there is a 2002 OP raising the age of children's protection from armed conflict from fifteen to eighteen; another 2002 OP expanding children's rights to protection against sale, forced labor, and sexual exploitation; and a 2011 OP clarifying how the CRC is implemented. Other OPs will doubtless follow, much as the US Constitution allows for new amendments.

The fight continues also to secure ratification of the CRC by its one remaining holdout, the United States. As mentioned, the United States played a leading role in drafting the CRC, and it has in fact "signed" it, but it has not taken the final step of "ratifying" it as part of US treaty law.

Opponents of US ratification fall into three general categories: (1) Some claim that the CRC is antifamily and would undermine parents' rights to raise and discipline children according to parents' own values. For example, children might gain freedoms to oppose parental wishes in divorce cases. (2) Others simply oppose ratifying UN treaties in general as threats to US sovereignty, and they also point out that US family law is chiefly governed not by the treaty-bound federal government but by individual states. (3) And some are opposed to specific CRC articles that would conflict with US law. For example, article 37.a bans children's sentencing to life imprisonment, which many US states permit (as well as children's capital punishment, which the United States only banned in 2005). Article 37.b might require minors to have standing to be heard in US courts. Article 28.1.b provides for universal secondary education, which may contravene the 1972 Supreme Court decision in *Wisconsin v. Yoder* that upheld Amish parents' rights to keep their children out of high school. Article 32 would call into question certain US labor laws that permit exemptions for children as young as twelve to work long hours in agriculture. And the CRC's OP on armed conflict could challenge US practices of adolescent recruitment into the armed forces.

Those pressing for US ratification of the CRC respond as follows. (1) Parents' rights are specifically protected in seven CRC articles (articles 5, 9, 14, 16, 18, 19, and 27), guaranteeing such things as that "states parties shall respect the rights and duties of parents" and that children cannot be separated from parents except in cases of abuse. (2) Not ratifying treaties like the CRC not only hampers efforts to improve children's rights in the United States but also places the United States in a weak position in the world, undermining its authority to address children's concerns in other countries. (3) And like all countries, the United States can ratify the CRC with any number of specific reservations it wishes to make to specific rights it finds objectionable. In addition, the CRC is not self-executing, meaning that it does not become a country's law by itself but only indirectly by generating discussion about the areas in which children's rights law and policy might be improved.

CONCLUSION: TOWARD WHAT FUTURE?

Where does the children's rights movement stand today and where might it go in the future?

The first wave, focusing on children's rights to a childhood, is now quite firmly established around the world. Few would not support children's provision rights to an education, health care, relief from poverty, and a family. There is disagreement about how extensive such rights should be. And clearly they are very often far from being fulfilled in reality. But the idea is largely accepted that basic provisions of children's welfare are responsibilities not just of private families and communities, as historically thought, but also of public agencies and governments.

The second wave has also powerfully changed worldwide opinion. Few any longer oppose children's protection rights such as against sexual abuse, armed violence, labor exploitation, and racial, ethnic, and gender discrimination. Sometimes protection rights are contested in particular cultural contexts. Sometimes they are not prioritized to the extent necessary. Often they are not implemented in practice because of significant obstacles of adult power, market exploitation, and government inaction. But it remains true nonetheless that governments, NGOs, judiciaries, and communities around the world strive to protect children from harm, and not just out of a sense of generosity but as a matter of human rights.

The third wave of children's participation rights is still relatively new and more controversial. Increasing numbers of children and child advocates are embracing the right of young people to exercise freedoms, agency, voices, and citizenship in public life. Children and youth are gaining new powers to influence public affairs and policies. Nevertheless, even the idea of children's participatory rights is often contested. Adults in general are still generally assumed to hold far greater rights to speak, act, and have an influence in the public realm. For example, almost no one under the age of eighteen can vote, an issue we look into in chapter 6.

Indeed, it could be said that one finds in this new wave of children's rights yet another kind of ambiguity. For while children's participation rights empower young people more fully than before to influence public life, these rights are almost always more limited than similar rights for adults and hence continue to disempower children anyway.

For example, CRC article 12.1, cited above, limits children's rights to freedom of expression in at least three ways: (1) only to "the child who is capable of forming his or her own views" and not all children; (2) only in "matters affecting the child" and not, as for adults, in all matters; and (3) only with "due weight in accordance with the age and maturity of the child," as presumably determined by adults. It could be argued that, in reality, men and women too are not completely capable of forming their own views and have capacities that evolve over time. But it would be unimaginable to limit their rights to free expression in such ways. There is again a double standard. Imagine substituting the word "woman" here for "child" and you can see the ambiguity.

This ambiguity deepens into a paradox when one considers that the basic purpose of participation rights is for participants to have the freedom to influence public affairs. If children's participatory rights are so freely limited and determined by adults, this arguably defeats the very purpose of having such rights in the first place. It is why children's public participation so often ends up merely tokenistic. Insofar as adults set the conditions for freedoms, adults (or select groups of adults) can maintain their own superior freedoms unchallenged. It is ultimately a question of power. Those holding power can structure societies in explicit and implicit ways that keep power from others.

This difficulty with children's participation rights has been recognized and addressed in a variety of ways.

One solution is to add what Mary John has called a "fourth P" to the three Ps under which children's rights are usually understood, a fourth P of "power." As, for example, street children and child parliamentarians in the Global South show, children are entirely capable of exercising power in the sense of "autonomy," or "realizing aspirations" that are "self-defined."[12] The lesson of the civil rights movements of women and other groups is that no one transcends second-class citizenship without achieving rights to exercise power on their own behalf. Children must have new rights to influence markets and economies, cultures and communities, and politics and policies. Only then will they will be able to transform public life in real and fundamental ways.

Another solution is to fully integrate child and youth rights into existing structures of adult rights. Ann Quennerstedt has argued that the very construction of children's rights under the three Ps sets children apart from the usual way that human rights are understood. This usual way is to divide rights according to a more historically rooted schema into civil, political, and social rights. Civil rights are freedoms of speech, conscience, religion, ownership, and the like. Political rights are opportunities to exercise political power. And social rights are entitlements to welfare, aid, and security.

Integrating children's rights into this broader framework would enforce fully equal rights standards. For example, there would no longer exist a special category of "protection" rights just for children that make children appear especially vulnerable and passive. In addition, participation rights would be replaced with the more specific and detailed categories of civil and political rights, requiring that children either be fully included or barred for good reasons. And changing provision rights into social rights, while essentially the same in content, "does not turn the child into a receiver to the same extent, but rather points towards the child's *access* to education or health care, or other social rights."[13] In short, the children's rights movement needs to reframe itself as part of the larger human rights movement instead of pursuing separate kinds of rights that inevitably leave children marginalized.

A third possible solution would be a childist one in which the children's rights movement transformed the larger discussion and practice of human rights as a whole. That is, the rights of the last major group to receive its rights would force upon societies an enlarged understanding of what rights are really all about for everyone. Perhaps, for example, instead of the three Ps being absorbed into civil, political, and social rights, the opposite would take place and adult rights would be rethought along the lines of the three Ps. For example, adults too would be understood as socially vulnerable and in need of systemic public protections. Or civil freedoms would no longer mean simple expressions of autonomy but rather means of interdependent public participation.

Only time will tell where the larger children's rights movement will eventually lead. But it is clear from the history sketched in this chapter that enormous change is possible. In less than two centuries, children's rights have emerged from complete obscurity to worldwide endorsement. They still have a very long way to go. But, as with the rights of other marginalized groups, the rights of children will reshape the rights and lives of us all.

4

EDUCATION IN AN AGE
OF GLOBALIZATION

The previous two chapters explored children's rights as a whole, from a theoretical and then a historical perspective. The next three chapters each examine in depth an important children's rights challenge for today. These particular examples—education, slavery, and voting rights—are but three of many possibilities. They are chosen as ways to highlight key issues surrounding, respectively, children's provision, protection, and participation rights. They all show that children's rights today remain challenges both *for* societies to think and act in new ways and *to* societies to move beyond their historically ingrained adultist biases.

The present chapter takes a look at one particularly telling illustration of this multidimensional challenge of children's rights—namely, education.

Education is one of the oldest and most settled of child and youth rights, yet it remains around the world today both contentious and far from universal. There is no nation on earth that does not endorse some kind of children's right to an education. Few argue against it and politicians and social reformers repeatedly champion it. But in reality, children in both poor and wealthy countries find their educational rights often severely limited. Millions of children receive no formal education at all. Millions more suffer from exceptionally poor educations or are discriminated against because of their gender, class, race, or ethnicity. Very few children on the planet have rights to make their own meaningful educational choices. And all too often, children's education is driven by ulterior political, cultural, or economic agendas that disregard children's own needs, experiences, and voices.

Consider again the famous case of the children's rights activist Malala Yousafzai. Yousafzai was awarded the 2014 Nobel Peace Prize for her work on behalf of girls' education in Pakistan, at age seventeen the youngest ever Nobel laureate. In 2009, at age eleven, Yousafzai had begun a blog sponsored by the BBC speaking out against the Taliban's rising suppression of children's and particularly girls' education rights in the Swat Valley. Yousafzai gradually rose to national and international prominence through her writings and interviews advocating for children's educational rights generally.

On the afternoon of October 9, 2012, she was approached by a Taliban gunman after she had boarded her school bus and shot three times, one bullet entering her forehead and almost killing her. After a protracted recovery, she continued her struggle for universal children's education, speaking at the United Nations, helping to create Pakistan's first Right to Education Bill, being featured in a documentary, cowriting a memoir, and continuing to this day to speak worldwide on the importance of education to all children without discrimination.

Yousafzai's case is just one vivid example of the issues surrounding children's educational rights. In this chapter we will limit ourselves to exploring five basic questions, all of them illustrated by Yousafzai's work. Is education a right at all? Should it be universal? Should it be equal? If it is a right, what is education a right to? And is there a right to educational choice? These questions can all be answered in different ways, and the answers affect not only theory and policy but also significant parts of children's everyday lives.

IS EDUCATION A RIGHT?

If one thinks about it, children have always, from prehistoric times to the present, received some kind of at least informal education. If education is defined as being taught the skills and knowledge needed to succeed in one's society, it is something that parents, communities, and cultures have almost always taken great pains to provide. Children and youth have almost always been taught to speak, get along with others, perform household duties, cook, work, contribute to their community, and much else. Many children over history have also learned to read and write, make a home and raise children, work in a trade or profession, and take part in cultural and political life. Long before anybody conceived of the idea of rights—and certainly long before there was any discussion of the rights of children—children have in fact been thought of as owed some kind of general moral entitlement to an education.

Is anything added, then, by thinking of education as a "right"?

Formally speaking, the right to an education belongs to what we have found is the oldest type of explicit children's rights in history—namely, rights to the provision of public support and aid. Provision rights (sometimes called survival and development rights) are rights to receive basic resources from one's society. Other forms of provision rights today, as we have seen, include rights to survival, health care, economic security, a family, play and leisure, a name and a nationality, disability support, and aid in times of distress. Some of the earliest children's rights laws in history provided children with educational opportunities. In the early twentieth century, it was provision rights to schooling, economic security, and relief aid that turned the children's rights movement into a truly global phenomenon.

To call education a "right" today is to say that it is not only desirable that children obtain it but also a public obligation of societies to provide it. It implies also that education ought as far as possible to be provided universally and without discrimination. Historically, children of wealthier and more powerful families received vastly superior educations to children whose families happened to be poor or marginalized. Indeed, most children throughout history received no formal education whatsoever. The movement to make education a "right" began and continues as a movement to ensure that a needed level and quality of education is available and accessible to all.

As Yousafzai found, however, such a right is still far from having been realized.

Globally, fifty-eight million children aged six to eleven (or 9 percent of all children that age) plus sixty-three million youth aged twelve to fifteen (or 13 percent) are not enrolled in any formal schooling at all. The highest percentage of children six to eleven who are out of school is in Africa (20 percent), followed by South America (7 percent), North America (6 percent), Asia (5 percent), and Europe (2 percent). Girls aged six to eleven are 12 percent more likely than boys not to be in school (though for girls aged twelve to fifteen, that figure falls to 1 percent).[1]

In addition, there continue to be vast discrepancies in educational effectiveness. For example, the global literacy rate for fifteen- to twenty-four-year-olds is only 89 percent. This breaks down regionally into 73 percent in Africa, 91 percent in Asia, 98 percent in North and South America, and 99 percent in Europe. While a great improvement upon history, these rates leave significant segments of humanity outside the global educational mainstream.

Another measure of education rights is percentage of GDP spent on child and youth education per country. Here we find a wide range again: from, for example, a low of 2.6 percent of GDP in Uganda, to 3.3 percent in India, 3.5 percent in China, 4.1 percent in Russia, 4.3 percent in Iran, 5.4 percent in the United States, 6.3 percent in the United Kingdom and Argentina, and a high of 7.0 percent in Sweden.[2] Although the reasons for not adequately funding education vary greatly, from the perspective of children themselves, a lack of educational resources generally translates into diminished rights to educational access and quality.

While there is no country in the world where children do not, therefore, officially have some rights to an education, the reality is that education rights vary greatly according to where one happens to have been born, one's gender, family income, cultural attitudes, and much else. Progress has been made since the pre–children's rights era, but not as much progress as one might expect. It is still necessary, therefore, to understand what truly makes education a "right" and why this right so often falls short of its potential.

IS THE RIGHT TO EDUCATION UNIVERSAL?

Carlos Nava is a ten-year-old boy living in Brazil's second-most populous state, Minas Gerais, birthplace of Brazil's former president Dilma Rousseff. His country has grown into the world's fifth-largest economy, yet it also has one of the world's widest income distributions. Nava attends school full-time and goes home at night to his parents, but like approximately half of all children in the state (in which half of the population is under eighteen), he also works outside school hours to support himself and his family. In Nava's case, he begs on the streets most weekdays before and after school and joins older children on weekends selling small products to tourists.

In Brazil, children have the right to a free and compulsory education from ages six to fourteen, as well as free but noncompulsory education up to age seventeen. However, in Minas Gerais, children like Nava who have to work usually drop out of school beginning at around age twelve and rarely complete high school.[3]

Such conditions, shared by so many of the world's children, half of whom live in poverty, raise the question of what it might mean to call education rights universal.

Universality can be defined in terms of both availability and access. As the education rights activist Katarina Tomasevski describes it in her position as Special Rapporteur of the United Nations Commission on Human Rights, children should have a "4-A" scheme of rights in which education is, all at once, available, accessible, acceptable, and adaptable.[4] Availability refers to making education a legal possibility for all children, and access refers to making it also a realistic option regardless of poverty and other hindrances. (The other two A's concern issues of quality and choice that we examine later.)

Putting aside extreme views such as those of the Pakistani Taliban, there is in fact significant debate about whether children's education is or should be available and accessible to all.

In terms of availability, for example, what ages count as universal? Only children in primary school? Children up to fourteen, as in Brazil? Or all children up to eighteen? Does this right include preschool? Could it include university? And are there legitimate ways in which educational availability may differ for girls and boys, wealthy and poor, and children of different ethnicities?

Even more complicated are questions of access. Does a universal education right mean that schooling must be free? So that children like Nava, for example, are able to stay in school? Does it depend on further rights such as to government support of poor families? Is the right to educational access violated if, for example, as in many developing countries, families with few resources are charged school fees? Or in some wealthier countries, if different schools are funded at significantly different levels? Or if extra funding is not made available to include children with disabilities or special needs?

Finally, what if education rights conflict with other kinds of fundamental rights? Should education be compulsory, for example, for children who need instead to work in order to survive? For children in war zones for whom it would be dangerous to leave their home? For adolescent girls in traditional cultures who wish instead to marry? For children or their families who have religious objections, such as the previously mentioned Amish in the United States?

International law has reached an official consensus on these issues. The consensus is that all children have a right to a free and compulsory education at least through primary school, and older children have a right to a secondary school education insofar as economically feasible.

This consensus emerged initially out of the UN's 1966 International Covenant on Economic, Social and Cultural Rights, which declares in article 13 that "primary education shall be compulsory and available free to all" and secondary education "made generally available and accessible to all." The 1989 CRC's article 28 requires along similar lines that countries "make primary education compulsory and available free to all" and "encourage the development of different forms of secondary education . . . [that are] available and accessible to every child." Most recently, the second of the UN's eight Millennium Development Goals, formulated in 2000 with the aim of eradicating global poverty, is to "ensure that, by 2015, children everywhere, boys and girls alike, will be able to complete a full course of primary schooling."

One or more of these agreements has been ratified by every nation in the world. In addition, as of 2011, 81 percent of countries' constitutions guaranteed children's rights to a primary education, and 37 percent guaranteed a secondary education for children up to between fourteen and eighteen years of age.[5] In Russia, for example, education is free and compulsory from ages seven to eighteen, but youth can leave school after fifteen with the approval of a parent and the local authority. In the United States, education is free and compulsory, but ages vary by state, with starting ages ranging from five to eight and ending ages ranging from fifteen to eighteen (with some states allowing early leave with parental approval). However, only 53 percent of countries' constitutions require primary education to be provided without fees or charges.[6] In Haiti, for example, children have the right to a compulsory education from ages six to eleven, but public schools generally charge fees, with the result that 80 percent of children in fact attend often less expensive paid private schools.

The situation is especially complicated when it comes to educational access. A good example is India, the country with the highest number of children in the world. Article 45 of the Indian Constitution of 1950 directs that every child up to the age of fourteen receive a free and compulsory education.[7] After decades of failed implementation, India's parliament passed the Right to Education Act 2009, which, among other things, upgrades a free and compulsory education up to age fourteen into a "fundamental right," meaning a right that supersedes all other rights; prohibits any fees, charges, or expenses that would prevent a child from attending; obliges local authorities to establish a school in their neighborhood and ensure registration and attendance; and provides funding for adequate numbers of teachers, proper infrastructure, and up-to-date pedagogical and disciplinary procedures.

Nevertheless, millions of Indian children still continue not to enroll in school. Indeed, the dropout rate since 2009 has actually increased. A large part of the problem is that poor families still need their children to work. Many cannot afford the fees or bribes that, contrary to the 2009 act, schools continue to levy. In addition, many schools are so vastly underresourced in terms of teachers, teacher pay, and infrastructure that attendance is not considered by many families to be worthwhile.[8]

The problem of providing a universal education exists to one degree or another in every country in the world. In poorer communities and countries, attending school is often unaffordable. As Tomasevski has argued, "The poverty of families, communities, and countries precludes access to education for many, if not most, unless education is free, namely provided or financed by the state."[9] In addition to the fifty-eight million children aged six to eleven (and sixty-three million aged twelve to fifteen) who do not attend school at all, many millions more attend only sporadically, lack qualified teachers, are not provided school buildings and supplies, do not have access to books or computers, and/or fail to grow up having attained basic levels of literacy.

The right to educational universality can also be problematic in cases of extraordinary educational expense. Some argue that disabled students, for example, do not have special rights to additional educational funding, since "pragmatically speaking, this financial burden is out of reach for most countries in the world, and communities would face severe burdens at the expense of other valuable social and political demands."[10] Universal education may not be a realistic ideal given that education is always relative to other social, economic, and cultural imperatives.

Against such realities, however, some argue that education is so fundamental a human right and so necessary for success in life that a universal right to education should be maintained as the goal.

Aman Ullah claims, for example, that it is up to societies rather than families to make universal education a reality. "Activist judges, civil society, media and academicians must play a sustainable vigilant role to make [the right to an education] a reality for the poor masses of Pakistan and India, who cannot afford their children's primary education."[11] Tomasevski places a universal obligation not only on nations but also on the international community. She argues for "an immediate and all-encompassing global commitment to eliminate the financial obstacles that impede free education for all school age children."[12] To call education a "right," by this view, is to hold local, national, and global actors accountable for making it as universally available and accessible as possible.

SHOULD EDUCATION BE EQUAL?

My office at Rutgers University is a little over a mile from Camden High School, which in 2014 was ranked as the very worst of all 339 high schools in the state of New Jersey.[13] Statistically, of course, every state has to have its lowest-performing educational institution. However, the depths of the problem at Camden High are staggering. In 2013, only 49 percent of its seniors graduated, compared to 93 percent of seniors nationwide. On that year's national SAT test, only 3 out of 882 juniors, or 0.3 percent, scored high enough to be considered college-ready, versus 43 percent nationwide.[14] Only 54 percent of Camden Public Schools' core academic classes are taught by highly qualified teachers, as compared to 95 percent across the state.[15] In addition, the school's infrastructure is so poor that many classrooms have no heating, and students and teachers have to wear coats and thermal underwear indoors.[16]

Gross inequalities of this kind mean that while some US students receive stellar educations, many receive profoundly inadequate ones. Indeed, US educational attainment is among the most unequal in the developed world and, on average, is lower than in almost every other wealthy country.

Why such a poor record in such a rich country?

The problem arguably comes down to racial and class segregation. The city of Camden's population is 95 percent African American or Hispanic, compared to 29 percent in the United States overall. Around 40 percent of the city's residents live below the poverty line, compared to 16 percent nationally. Children in cities like Camden are subject to intense police scrutiny and zero-tolerance disciplinary systems, resulting in a well-documented "school-to-prison pipeline" that incarcerates African American youth at six times the rate of whites.[17] In many communities like Camden in the United States, three out of four young black men have served time in prison.[18] Discriminatory laws on crime and drugs combined with lack of economic opportunities contribute to a crime rate in Camden that is 6.6 times the national average.[19] The reality is that if you happen to be born in a racially and economically segregated community such as Camden, your educational opportunities are profoundly diminished and the wider society does not step in to make up much of the difference.

Educational inequality is not just a US problem but also a problem worldwide. In poorer countries, governments often provide few subsidies, resulting in the most impoverished children—and especially girls—receiving the least schooling or no schooling at all. In rapidly emerging economies, such as Brazil, Russia, India, and China, the inequalities, if anything, are even sharper, as wealthier classes can now afford increasingly expensive schools while poorer classes fall further and further behind. Even in Europe, where educational equality is relatively high, gains made in the mid-twentieth century are now being rolled back by cuts in state funding.

What could it mean, then, under conditions such as these, to have a right to educational equality? There are two somewhat conflicting possible answers to this question.

First, educational equality could mean the right to the same minimum level of educational opportunities.

This equal opportunities approach lies behind, for example, the CRC and Millennium Development Goals of every child's right to a mandatory and free education at least up through primary school. According to Tomasevski, equal opportunities must be secured against the privatizing forces of global marketplaces. "The key facet of globalization, liberalization, is predicated on increasing the privatization of education, which demands decreased involvement of the state. . . . [In response,] international human rights law mandates state intervention, requiring it to ensure, at least, free and compulsory education for all children."[20] The right to an equal education is the right for each child to be provided with sufficient public resources to gain the same level of basic skills and knowledge.

This approach has arguably resulted in significant educational gains over the past two to three decades. UNESCO reports that "between 1999 and 2011, the number of children out of school fell almost by half," and "the proportion [of countries] reaching universal primary enrolment rose from 30% in 1999 to 50% in 2011." In addition, the world is closer to achieving primary school equality for girls.[21] The recently created Human Development Index finds that "poor countries [since 1970 are] rapidly catching up on aggregated educational attainment and gender equality but not necessarily on quality."[22] It must also be noted, however, that this progress has somewhat stagnated since about 2004, which UNESCO ascribes to a drop-off in international funding and an increase in global armed conflicts.[23]

A second approach focuses instead not on equal educational opportunities but on equal educational empowerment.

Educational empowerment here means cultivating children's own diverse and locally based agency and voices. It replaces a top-down imposition of adult-oriented outcomes with a bottom-up investment in child-oriented capabilities. On a global scale, it resists Western-dominated aid regimes in favor of supporting local educational cultures.

One problem with the equal opportunity model, according to this view, is that it often leads to education's overly burdensome top-down standardization. For example, the recent US experiment called No Child Left Behind imposed such a strong and punitive system of testing on children that, in the name of equality of outcomes, it greatly diminished children's own educational agency. As a result, poorer schools that rely more heavily on federal funding were compelled by federal rules to focus their curricula on a narrow set of testable information, with the ironic result that poorer children ended up with even worse educational outcomes. Similarly, according to Rhys Griffith, standardization tends to emphasize passively acquired knowledge over the harder to measure but more important skills of "global citizens" who are "critically reflective, morally autonomous and socially active."[24]

In contrast, the equal empowerment approach starts with local cultures. For example, indigenous Maya children in Mexico successfully freed their schools from national standards that did not make sense to their communities. "School subjects are [now] derived from ethnic lore and collective memory," with the result, as one young person puts it, that "autonomy means that we are going to construct our own education."[25] As another example, some rural schools in Sudan blend formal schooling with informal learning in children's everyday lives, such as on the family farm or in the family business.[26] Poorer students actually learn more because their schooling grows organically out of their own lived experiences.

This approach also claims to help fight larger social inequalities. For example, some Nigerian schools are giving a greater voice to girls. According to one study, "Realizing [an equal] education [in Nigeria] is not simply about enrolling equal numbers of girls and boys in school . . . [but about] how gendered relations in school have resonance with those in the labour market, with patterns of ownership of assets, [and] the distribution of power in the political, cultural, and social sphere."[27] Girls are encouraged to use the classroom to discuss and confront gender disparities in the larger society. One could speak in this regard of fostering educational "friction": enabling girls and other marginalized groups to use schooling to investigate deep societal norms.[28]

There are pros and cons to both of these approaches to educational equality. The equal opportunities approach rightly encourages governments and the international community to do their best to provide all children with basic educational resources and attainment. But it tends to override local cultural differences and children's own agency and experiential realities. The equal empowerment approach rightly focuses on cultivating children's own individual and culturally diverse capacities. But it cannot succeed if schools lack the minimum resources needed to invest in every child's success.

WHAT IS EDUCATION A RIGHT TO?

Often lost in the discussion of children's education rights is a further question: what exactly is education a right to? However universally or equally, what should the right to an education concretely provide?

There are at least three possible answers to this question. One emphasizes children's rights to quality teachers; another to gaining socially productive skills; and another still to cultivating student-centered critical thinking. Of course, these options are not mutually exclusive. But differences in emphasis can change how education is actually experienced as a right in the classroom.

UNESCO is an example of an organization that comes down primarily in the camp of children's right to quality teachers. As its

2013–14 report, *Teaching and Learning: Quality for All*, puts it, "An education system is only as good as its teachers . . . [and] education quality improves when teachers are supported—it deteriorates if they are not." The right to a quality education is a right primarily to quality teachers who are professionals able to decide what is best for each classroom and student.

To this end, UNESCO identifies four key strategies for providing all students the best possible teachers: that teachers "reflect the diversity of the children they will be teaching"; that teachers are "trained to support the weakest learners"; that the best teachers are allocated to "the most challenging parts of the country"; and that teachers are provided "the right mix of incentives to encourage them to remain in the profession." UNESCO estimates that these goals require twenty-six billion dollars more of investment in education than is currently made worldwide.[29]

A strength of this approach is its focus on teaching professionalism. In much of the world, teachers are not well trained or supported. This view is also highly responsive to local educational cultures and hence to children's own particular situations and experiences. A drawback, however, is affordability. Many communities lack even basic resources for health and survival and can little afford extensive educational investment. And even wealthier countries will have to make special efforts to funnel the best teachers into the least advantaged communities.

A second approach is to focus on providing children the skills they need to become socially productive adults. The right to an education is the right to whatever basic knowledge and abilities are needed to succeed in the larger world.

One example would be the already mentioned US focus on standardized testing. The United States has long used tests such as the Scholastic Aptitude Test (SAT), taken at around age seventeen, to help direct formal schooling toward the development of basic linguistic and mathematical "aptitudes" needed for a productive adulthood. Similarly, South Korea has produced one of the highest-performing education systems in the world through its rigorous College Scholastic Ability Test, which is so competitive that students and their families devote significant time and money to doing well on it. Children have the right to be held to high standards.

This approach has the advantage of being able to define a quality education in broad societal terms. Education policymakers can use the latest pedagogical research to direct schooling toward ends that children will find socially useful. And, in theory at least, common standards can encourage greater educational equality. But focusing too heavily on outcomes is potentially disempowering for both teachers and children. Teachers may be discouraged from exercising their own creativity in the classroom. And children may find it harder to connect their educations with their own experiences and cultures. Education is primarily directed toward external adult goals instead of internal child agency. Finally, an outcomes approach is only as good as the system it creates. South Korea is relatively successful because high-stakes testing is accompanied by one of the highest percentages of GDP invested in education in the world. The United States, in contrast, couples high-stakes testing with relatively low investment in schools, with the result, as former assistant secretary of education Diane Ravitch has argued, that real educational outcomes have consequently worsened.[30]

A third approach is to emphasize children's rights to develop their own capacities and critical thinking. This approach is student centered rather than teacher centered or adult centered. It is focused on children's empowerment as children with their own interests, experiences, and aims.

Such an emphasis can be found, for example, in the highly effective education systems of Finland and Sweden. According to one study, "In Swedish policy, student influence is highlighted as the most important of all children's rights issues in education. The political documents clearly state that children in early childhood education and in school have the right to participate in public will formation and decision-making (in school) and to influence activities, learning content and methods." This study also suggests that "a student's right to influence is connected to the promotion of democratic values and the education of the democratic citizen: children shall be given the opportunity to practice democracy in a democratic environment."[31] The central children's right here is for children themselves to participate in meaningfully directing their own educations. In Finland, often considered to have the very highest-achieving educational system in the world, students are subjected to very few standardized tests, have significant time for recreation and play, and have high levels of choice over the subjects they study.

Perhaps the chief benefit of this approach is that it treats children not as preadults but as educational agents in their own right. In addition, by focusing on the goals of children themselves instead of teachers or societies, children are empowered to connect their educations to their own local cultures. A disadvantage is that this approach can succeed only when coupled with high public investment in educational resources. There need, for example, to be low teacher-to-student ratios. In addition, self-empowerment might work more effectively in less culturally diverse societies in which general educational standards are already implicitly shared.

All three children's rights advocated for here are important: quality teachers, productive outcomes, and student empowerment. The question is not which aim should be chosen but which aim should be prioritized. Especially when there are scarce resources.

Nevertheless, one can draw a couple of general conclusions.

First, merely creating strict educational standards does not work. It ignores other important children's rights such as to quality teachers and student empowerment. And it imposes a top-down power structure that undermines students' and teachers' educational energies and creativity. Educational standards are no substitute for investments of educational resources.

And second, national and global education policies need to pay more attention to children's rights to direct their own educational experiences. Children are not merely preadults but active thinkers and citizens in their own right. Consequently, quality teaching and high standards must ultimately connect to children's own abilities, lives, and experiences. In other words, whatever else education is a right to, it should involve the right to children's empowerment as children.

IS THERE A RIGHT TO EDUCATIONAL CHOICE?

New Zealand elementary schools have a creative way of assessing themselves. They ask students to use digital media such as writing, photos, pictures, and videos to create "learning stories" of their own academic progress. These learning stories describe students' academic interests, levels of involvement, engagement with new challenges, persistence in the face of difficulties, and ability to take responsibility. They are used in conjunction with teachers' corresponding "teaching stories" to help students, teachers, and parents reflect on what the child has learned and where he or she might go in the future. The idea was inspired by the CRC's participation rights under the auspices of New Zealand's new Early Childhood Curriculum Guidelines (known as *Te Whāriki*), created in 1996. The children's learning stories aim to incorporate "a respect for children and children's voice into early childhood education" and to treat children as "active learners who choose, plan, and challenge."[32]

This example raises a final question that we will consider: what rights should children and youth have to participate in making educational choices?

This question spans a range of potential controversies: Is there a right to avoid formal schooling altogether, and, if so, does it apply to all children and youth or only before and after certain ages? Is there a right for children to choose where to attend school, such as outside their district or in private, religious, or home schooling? Within any particular educational structure, should children have a right to participate in school governance, for example, in helping design curricula, participating in assessing outcomes, running meaningful school councils, or influencing such things as sports choices and lunch options? And within the classroom, what rights might children have to take part in shaping their own learning and activities on a day-to-day basis?

The traditional and still dominant view worldwide is that children's rights to participate in educational choices should be quite limited. It is thought that precisely because of children's lack of education, their educational choices should generally be made by adults. This view goes back to Locke's idea that children develop only in stages, with full competence being reached only upon a future fully formed adulthood.

Following upon the growth of the childhood studies movement in the 1980s, however, scholars and policymakers have increasingly tried to understand what it might mean for children and youth to have rights to participate in educational choices for themselves. No one is arguing that children should have completely free rein (or, for that matter, that parents, teachers, or school administrators should either). But it is also clear that children and youth do and can exercise educational agency in the classroom, the school, and the community. The argument is increasingly made that children should not lose their basic human rights to agency and a voice when they step into school.

There are basically two arguments for children's participation rights in education, one instrumental and the other intrinsic.

First, the instrumental argument is that children's free participation in their own educations improves educational outcomes. CRC article 29 asserts that children's education "shall be directed to," among other things, "the development of respect for human rights and fundamental freedoms" and "the preparation of the child for responsible life in a free society." It is difficult to see how children will develop respect for fundamental freedoms and responsible decision making without being able to exercise such freedoms in the school setting. An education that suppresses children's thinking and voices is unlikely to produce thinking and deliberative citizens.

In addition to the above examples from Sweden, Finland, and New Zealand, children's educational agency is also being supported in parts of Brazil. Here, "early opportunities for democratic participation [in education] nourish a sense of collective ownership and responsibility . . . [and] a belief in themselves as actors who have the power to impact the adverse conditions that shape their lives."[33] Within the classroom, democratic knowledge and skills might be enhanced by including Socratic methods in which students are treated as active and engaged learners. Beyond the classroom, students are likely to develop higher levels of engagement and enthusiasm if they can participate in public discussions of educational policy.

Second, the intrinsic argument for children's rights to educational choices is that children in school deserve to be treated with full dignity and respect. As Ann Quennerstedt puts it, "The relations between adults and children, and between children, have to be infused with human rights values, as must the learning situation itself. This means that the very heart of education, i.e. the processes in which educational content, methods of teaching and evaluation of education are formed and carried out, have to invite and respect children as rightful participants in the entire learning process."[34] Following CRC articles 12 and 13, children have rights in any setting to freedom of expression and freedom of information as matters of equal human dignity.

The complexity of the matter here can be illustrated by children's school councils. The purpose of children electing their peers to represent them in school councils is generally to provide children a voice in educational matters and policies. But children themselves, when interviewed, typically find their school councils to be ineffective and tokenistic.[35] While the vast majority of students in New Zealand secondary schools believe that their views should be taken into account, only about a third believe they actually are.[36] Council representatives might hold open and serious discussions on issues ranging from playground equipment to adequate lighting and heating, from bullying to drugs, from courses offered to complaints about requirements. But, in the end, school councils rarely have much power to enact changes. Their recommendations are almost always filtered through adult advisors and administrators.

It could also be helpful to distinguish different possible levels of children's participatory rights in education. Roger Hart and Harry Shier have developed a model for assessing children's participatory rights in general, called a "ladder of participation." Shier's most recent version distinguishes five increasing steps: (1) children are "listened to"; (2) they are "supported in expressing their views"; (3) their views "are taken into account"; (4) they are "involved in decision-making processes"; and (5) at the highest level, they "share power and responsibility for decision-making."[37]

In this model, school councils appear typically stuck at level 2, where children are supported in expressing their views but those views are not generally taken into account in actual policies. The "learning stories" that we started out with, however, arguably move further up to level 4 or even 5, since students here are actively involved in the decision-making process and even per-haps share in making decisions about how to move forward.

It is not possible for anyone in any setting to have complete freedom over their choices. But the question for children is how their educational choices may become respected and meaningful. In part it is a question of power. Education has traditionally been understood as an arena in which children are empowered for their futures as adults rather than in their present as children. Children's rights to exercise educational choices for themselves face deeply entrenched adult privileges to exercise educational agency and expertise. The reality, however, is that no one, child or adult, is ever completely educated and learning is a lifelong pro-cess for us all. In one way or another, children too deserve rights not only to be provided an education but also to participate ac-tively in directing it.

CONCLUSION

The present chapter has looked into some of the more basic ques-tions surrounding children's education rights, from whether edu-cation is a right at all to the extent to which it should be universal and equal, what education might be a right to, and how much children are owed educational choices. There are, of course, many other education rights questions, such as whether disabled students have a right to inclusive schooling, the extent to which children should have rights to override the wishes of their par-ents, whether formal education rights should also be extended to adults, and how education is related to other children's rights, such as to economic security, work, and health.

Although education is usually thought about as a provision right, it turns out, as we have seen, that it is also a protection and a participation right. Education involves protections against dis-crimination, exploitation, and abuse. And it rests on rights to freedom of expression, cultural inclusion, and participation. Indeed, viewed solely as a provision right, education can defeat its own purposes by treating children merely as objects of adult beneficence instead of also as subjects who are empowered to learn.

Education rights are less about saving children's childhoods than about investing in children's capacities and empowering children as children.

5

THE NEW CHILD SLAVERY

You might be surprised to find a chapter in this book on child slavery. Wasn't slavery abolished long ago? Isn't it obvious that child slavery in particular is one of the grossest of human rights violations? What is there to discuss?

All true. Unfortunately, however, child slavery is in fact a significant problem in every country in the world today and by some estimates is on the rise. With globalization, it has become easier for corporations and businesses to evade national antislavery laws that were built up over the past two centuries as well as for children in particular to be trafficked as slaves across borders. While the enslavement of young people under eighteen is illegal in all countries and banned also under a century of international antislavery conventions, it has become, if anything, easier to exploit vulnerable populations like children for their slave labor.

Today child slavery takes place in all corners of the world: from tobacco farming in Eastern Europe to domestic servitude in Western Europe; from factory exploitation in East Asia to forced soldiering in West Africa; from drug trafficking in Central America to prostitution in North America. The question is not whether child slavery exists today. The questions are why it persists, how it has changed, and whether it is possible to come up with new solutions adequate to its new global realities.

The International Labour Organization (ILO) estimates that there are approximately 5.5 million child slaves working around the world today. These include 3,780,000 in forced labor, 960,000 in sexual exploitation, 709,000 enslaved by states, and 300,000 in child soldiering.[1] Depending on how it is defined, others have put the figure of overall child slavery much higher, at over twenty-seven million.[2] Free the Slaves estimates that there are currently around fifteen thousand minors working in slavery conditions in the United States, chiefly in prostitution and drug trafficking, but also in domestic servitude, farming, and factories.[3] The Anti-Slavery Society claims that while minors make up a third of the world population, they make up at least half of all slaves. And while it has recently leveled off, child slavery rose significantly over the past several decades.[4]

Child slavery is usually thought about as violating rights to protection. Protection rights in general are rights against being done harm by others or groups. They include protections against all kinds of abuse, violence, discrimination, and exploitation. They are often the first rights one thinks of when one thinks of children's rights, as their violation can be obvious and dramatic. Indeed, it was in part protections against slave-like working conditions that started the entire children's rights movement in the early nineteenth century.

Nevertheless, just as with education, child slavery involves other kinds of rights too. It is also an issue of children's rights to provision and participation. Child slavery arises in part from a lack of adequate provision rights such as to education and economic security; and it involves violating participation rights such as to freedoms of movement and speech. As a result, child slavery, again like education, is a matter not just of child saving but also of child empowerment.

Under conditions of globalization, child slavery involves us all. As we have seen, there are many kinds of labor that can be useful and even necessary for children to be involved in. But there continue to exist forms of child labor that are forced, exploitative, or hazardous. Such labor is woven throughout the new global economic order: in the clothes we wear, the food we eat, and the technologies we use. It is built into problems of illegal immigration, drug trafficking, civil war, and terrorism. Child slavery is one of the most vital and complex issues raised by our increasingly interconnected global lives.

This chapter explores the following basic questions: What is child slavery? What practices might it include? What is the impact of globalization? When does child labor become truly exploitative? How can child slavery be addressed through law? And how is it an issue of broader human rights?

WHAT IS CHILD SLAVERY?

The most common kind of child slavery in the United States is in sex work, involving an estimated three hundred thousand US-born minors and seventeen thousand trafficked from abroad, 90 percent of them girls.[5] Most adult prostitutes began as minors. A former child prostitute in the United States describes how she became involved in the business:

> I was 14 years old, and the way the pimp came at me was that at first I didn't even know he was a pimp. He came at me like a boyfriend. Yes, he was an older boyfriend but he cared about me. . . . Six months later he told me 'Let's run away together. We can have a beautiful house and family.' And I did believe him, and we ran away, and then the story changed and I met the other girls that he had in his stable. And I had to go out every night and work the streets—the alternative was being gang-raped by a group of pimps while everyone watched.[6]

Both US and international law consider all child sex work to be child slavery, on account of its being intrinsically exploitative. US federal law prohibits all aspects of minors' sex work: transportation for sexual purposes, sexual coercion or enticement, sex trafficking, sexual exploitation, sale or buying for sex, and use in pornography or obscene visual representation.[7] Children perform sex work in brothels, through pimps, via the Internet, on the streets, and sometimes through family members. As an example of this last type, a man was prosecuted in federal court in Kansas City for driving around selling his fourteen-year-old stepdaughter to adult men for sex.[8]

What exactly turns child labor into child slavery? The answer is more complicated than one might think.

The international human rights community would consider the fourteen-year-old prostitute in our example a child slave on various counts: she is forced into her work, exploited by adults, exposed to significant hazards, and not realistically able to leave. This definition of slavery is different from the nineteenth-century definition with which most of us are more familiar, that is, the literal ownership of another human being for labor purposes. What it means to be enslaved has changed with the changing nature of the global economy. Today, the slavery of minors or adults rarely involves actual ownership and is instead typically characterized by labor being forced and exploitative.

We can see how and why this shift took place by looking at evolving international law. Almost a century ago, the world united to create the landmark 1926 Slavery Convention, intended to end slavery once and for all everywhere. But here slavery was defined in its nineteenth-century sense: "Slavery is the status or condition of a person over whom any or all of the powers attaching to the right of ownership are exercised."[9] Slavery equals ownership.

However, as early as 1930, the ILO began to realize that persons could be enslaved in other ways. Its Forced Labour Convention No. 29, now ratified by 174 nations, defined slavery instead as any manner of "forced labour," meaning "all work or service that is exacted from any person under the menace of any penalty and for which the said person has not offered himself voluntarily."[10] (There were some exceptions made, such as the forced labor of a military draft.) Likewise, the ILO's 1957 Abolition of Forced Labour Convention No. 105 sought to ban "any form of forced or compulsory labour."[11] The same language is found in article 8 of the UN's 1966 International Covenant on Civil and Political Rights (ICCPR), ratified by 167 nations, that legally binds signatory countries to outlaw both traditional ownership slavery and "forced or compulsory labour."[12]

Children and youth are not mentioned specifically in any of these international conventions, though neither are they excluded. The labor exploitation of children is not explicitly addressed until the ILO's 1973 Minimum Age Convention No. 138, now ratified by 154 nations. The focus here, however, is less on labor exploitation per se than on banning labor under the age of fifteen, the implication being that such labor is forced and exploitative by definition. It also calls for a ban on child labor at any age during which children have rights to compulsory schooling or that is "likely to jeopardise the health, safety or morals of young persons." A similar logic underlies, around the same time, two 1977 additional protocols to the 1949 Geneva Conventions that ban the use and recruitment of anyone into the armed forces under the age of fifteen.

Definitions shift again with the 1989 CRC. Here, children are to be protected under the broader concept of "economic exploitation." Article 32 requires that "States Parties recognize the right of the child to be protected from economic exploitation and from performing any work that is likely to be hazardous or to interfere with the child's education, or to be harmful to the child's health or physical, mental, spiritual, moral or social development." The

CRC further prohibits a variety of specific exploitative labor practices: the use of children in prostitution or pornography (article 34), children's sale or trafficking (article 35), and the recruitment of children under fifteen into armed conflict (article 38). These bans are further spelled out in two 2002 optional protocols to the CRC: on the sale of children, child prostitution, and child pornography and on the involvement of children in armed conflict.

Currently, the most definitive international agreement concerning child slavery is the ILO's 1999 Worst Forms of Child Labor Convention No. 182, ratified by 172 states. Here the concept of child labor exploitation is redefined even more broadly as "the worst forms of child labour." "Worst forms" is defined as encompassing children's ownership for labor, sale and trafficking, debt bondage, serfdom, forced or compulsory labor, compulsory recruitment into armed conflict, prostitution, pornography, drug trafficking, or any work likely to harm children's health, safety, or morals. While this definition may be vague, it has the benefit of encompassing a wide array of exploitative, harmful, and forced acts.

Outside of international law, the international NGO Free the Slaves defines slavery more simply as "being forced to work without pay, under the threat of violence, and being unable to walk away."[13] Labor is effectively slave-like, in this view, if one is prevented by force from leaving. One scholar defines child slavery more broadly still: "In today's world, de facto power and control rather than de jure ownership is the basis for assessing whether a particular child should be described as a child slave."[14] In other words, child slavery means any labor that is forced upon children by means of power and control.

It remains, therefore, not entirely clear how child slavery is to be defined. It could include any or all of the following: ownership for labor; labor exploitation; broader economic exploitation; performing labor that is harmful or hazardous; or being forced to work or prevented from leaving. The reason for these different definitions is that labor itself is in flux under its rapidly increasing globalization, which opens up diverse new ways to exploit children for work.

WHAT PRACTICES MIGHT CHILD SLAVERY INCLUDE?

Given these difficulties of general definition, it is instructive to drill down more specifically into what kinds of labor practices might be involved. While there remain differences, the international community largely agrees on a number of types of work from which children should have the right to be protected.

The most common form of child slavery worldwide is in domestic servitude. The ILO defines slave-like child domestic labor as "situations where children perform domestic tasks in the home of a third party of 'employer' under exploitative conditions (long working hours, with little or no wages, for example, or below the minimum working age)."[15] Children as young as five often work twelve to sixteen hours a day in a combination of tasks such as cooking, cleaning, caring for smaller children, gardening, and/or working on a family farm or business. The majority are girls. While there are no reliable statistics, the highest predominance is across Africa and South Asia, while thousands are also trafficked annually for household labor into Europe and the United States.[16]

Most child domestic servants come from deeply impoverished backgrounds, are paying off parental debts, lost their parents to AIDS or other illnesses, or are running away from an abusive home.[17] Some believe their work will lead to educational or employment benefits in the future. They usually lack access to education, however, and because they are isolated from public view can endure physical, mental, and sexual abuse. A child domestic servant in the Philippines reports, for example, that "they hurt me, spank me, throw things at me, use hurtful words."[18] Frequently children are locked in the home, prevented from contacting parents, provided no days off, and paid nothing or only enough to cover debts owed to owners or traffickers.[19]

Another large number of child slaves globally work in agriculture or industry. Many such children are abducted or trafficked. Others are trapped into exploitative labor by debt bondage, that is, working to pay off loans made to their parents. Others still are tricked into thinking they are being provided ordinary employment.

Tipu, for example, is a fourteen-year-old boy working for a fishery in Bangladesh. He had run away from an abusive stepfather only to be deceived by a slave recruiter and sold for around five hundred to eight hundred taka (ten to sixteen US dollars) to the local mafia. He works imprisoned with other boys on a slave island for sixteen to eighteen hours a day, often all night, sorting, cleaning, and drying fish while receiving no compensation besides small meals and a sleeping mat on the fishery floor. The fishery owners threaten the children with violence if they try to escape, and local police and officials are paid off to look the other way.[20]

Or consider eight-year-old Mohammed Sharif, who was abducted from his village in Nepal and sold for fifteen hundred Nepali rupees (twenty US dollars) to an embroidery factory owner in Mumbai, India. Here he works sixteen to eighteen hours a day, receives only minimal food, is never permitted to leave the factory, and is severely beaten if he breaks the rules. As he reports, "If I fall asleep they pour salt and chili powder in my eyes."[21]

Another significant form of child slavery is sex work, including prostitution, stripping, and participation in pornography. Some also consider sex work to include child marriage, with the view that it is necessarily forced due to a child's immaturity. Child sex work takes place worldwide, and the illegal sex industry overall is the third-largest global criminal enterprise behind trade in drugs and arms.[22] As already noted, prostitution is the most common form of child slavery in the United States. But child sex work is widespread around the world. In India, for example, there are thought to be anywhere from thirty-five thousand to five hundred thousand children, chiefly girls, currently engaged in sex work of one kind or another.[23]

Many children are forced into sex work by adults, and many are held captive by violence, drug addiction, or debt bondage. At the same time, some children take on sex work as a choice to support themselves or their families. In the United States, "at least 70 percent of women involved in prostitution were introduced into the commercial sex industry before reaching 18 years of age." Or, as a former US child prostitute stated: "We're all under 18. We're all the same age. There would be a few girls I knew who were in their 20s or whatever, but they were doing it since they were our age anyways. I did wait till 12, and these girls had been doing it since they were eight or nine and now they are like 23."[24] One study of girls trafficked out of Chicago shows that they are required to have sex with generally around ten to fifteen clients a night, or to bring in between five hundred and one thousand dollars a night, with the threat of violence or deprivation if they fail to meet quotas.[25]

Another practice often considered child slavery is child soldiering. There are estimated to be around three hundred thousand minors who are fighting in some form of armed conflict today, 70 percent of them boys.[26] Many children involved are conscripted and retained through forceful means such as violence, bribery, being drugged, becoming "wives" for other soldiers, being recruited into terrorism, or through lack of other viable alternatives. Many child soldiers, however, choose to fight of their own volition; for example, if their village is attacked or they believe in the cause they are fighting for. Nevertheless, all child soldiering is illegal under international law, and the UN and ILO view it along similar lines to sex work as inherently forced, exploitative, or harmful.

In addition, the UN and ILO consider numerous other forms of child labor to be slavery or slave-like. These include the estimated 1.2 million children in the world undergoing child trafficking, since children in the process of being transported illegally are generally also being exploited for third-party profit and forced not to escape.[27] Other children who may be considered to work in slave-like conditions are street beggars forced to give their profits to adult employers, serfs bonded to landowners, and children who traffic illegal drugs.[28]

WHEN IS CHILD LABOR EXPLOITATIVE?

Around fifteen hundred boys and girls aged twelve to seventeen work in the thriving shoe industry of the town of Franca, Brazil. They work in small household factories performing such tasks as cutting and sewing leather and gluing soles. Since about 25 percent of all shoes made in Franca are exported to the United States, the US government has led an international effort to enforce international standards and ban such child labor in Brazil, though so far with little success.[29] It argues that these children's labor is exploitative because it pays little, exposes children to harmful fumes, and keeps them from attending school.

An interview with a fourteen-year-old girl working in one of these household shoe factories highlights the complexity of the situation. As she says:

> They exploit you a lot; we work a lot and earn very little. . . .
> [However,] when you don't have anything better to do, it's
> what you do. No, no, I don't like it. I don't think anyone likes
> it, but they do it out of obligation. Some people do it to help
> their families. I, working, want to be more independent. But

they exploit people a lot. They really exploit. In the final analysis, people work a lot and the salaries are much lower than the
value of the work.[30]

This child worker refers explicitly to her own exploitation. Yet in
the same breath she also claims her right to choose this work for
herself, for a variety of economic, familial, and personal reasons.

What might make child labor "exploitative," and how might it
be distinguished from child labor that is ordinary or acceptable?
There are two broad ways to answer this question.

One way is to focus on the nature of the child labor itself.
From this perspective, child labor is exploitative if it violates children's dignity or basic interests. As the ILO's Minimum Age Convention No. 138 puts it, labor is exploitative if it undermines "the
fullest physical and mental development of young persons" (article 1) or is "likely to jeopardise the health, safety or morals of
young persons" (article 3). For example, a part-time job babysit-
ting or bussing tables at a restaurant is generally not exploitative
because it provides experience and rewards to young people without interfering with schooling and leisure. But work like in the
shoe industry in Franca may be termed exploitative because it
pays little, incurs health risks, and limits time spent on school.

This argument also includes labor that is forced or coerced.
Some view practically all paid child labor as forced and therefore
exploitative because children lack full capacities to consent to it.[31]
Others argue that children are simply more easily coerced than
adults. According to Sarah Murillo, "Children are less educated,
easily overpowered, and easily manipulated into doing what an
adult tells them to do."[32] Along these lines, the 2000 Palermo
Protocol to Prevent, Suppress and Punish Trafficking in Persons
Especially Women and Children generally defines child trafficking as exploitative because no child can rightly be said to have
consented voluntarily to such treatment.[33]

Another way to distinguish "exploitative" from acceptable child labor is to place the child's labor in its larger economic context. From this perspective, children's work is only exploitative if it creates worse conditions than the child would otherwise experience. A child farmer might otherwise starve. A child shoe factory worker might otherwise gain no marketable skills. A child prostitute might otherwise live homeless on the streets. Exploitation is relative to surrounding social conditions such as poverty and poor educational opportunities.

According to Lawrence French and Richard Wokutch, this means that child labor becomes exploitative only when it contravenes particular children's "opportunity to achieve their potential as human beings." Thus, "it is morally unacceptable for children to work in conditions that foreclose their opportunities for reaching that potential because the work precludes them from gaining a basic education, or because exposure to hazards on the job is likely to endanger the child's physical or psychological well-being." But, at the same time, children's labor should not be deemed exploitative if it "is critical to their survival and development"; if the "harm that children suffer in the workplace [is] outweighed by the advancement of their economic position and that of their families"; or if "difficulties in attending school may be offset by the work experience and skill development they gain in the workforce."[34]

Whether a child or child advocate considers labor exploitative, therefore, depends on how much weight is given to the intrinsic nature of the work itself versus the extrinsic social conditions surrounding it. Both are obviously relevant. Focusing on the work itself demands a more universal position that tries to eradicate all child labor that is harmful or forced. In contrast, accounting for larger economic conditions demands a more context-specific position that weighs child labor against other available opportunities.

WHAT IS THE IMPACT OF GLOBALIZATION?

The jacket you put on this morning might include fragments of cotton picked by an eleven-year-old in Pakistan, cloth woven by a six-year-old in Brazil, stitching performed by a four-year-old in Bangladesh, and dye made from chemicals harvested by a ten-year-old in Indonesia. According to Free the Slaves, "Slaves harvest cocoa in West Africa, and it ends up in our chocolate. Slaves make charcoal in Brazil, which is used to run smelters that make steel for our cars. Many food products and raw materials are tainted by slavery—such as tomatoes, tuna, shrimp, cotton, diamonds, iron, sugar, and gold."[35] Child slaves are employed in the United States to harvest sugar for breakfast cereal.

Child slavery is not a separate problem for other people around the world but enmeshed in every aspect of today's global economy. It is built into the food we eat, the raw materials that go into our products, and virtually any technology or good we might use. No one can honestly say that they are not touched by child slavery in one way or another.

All of this is because of the nature of twenty-first-century globalization. Globalization means that local activities are deeply interconnected around the world. Labor and resources from around the planet are combined together all at once in almost every product we use. Even if you buy only locally grown food, you do not know who made the cardboard box it comes in, the parts in the car that transports it, the components of the computer on which you order it, and so on without end.

What is more, while companies that employ child slaves can sometimes be identified, it is difficult to track down most products' entire production process from raw materials to users. Equally difficult to assess are the impacts, negative and positive, of child slavery on the global economy itself, where, for example, it may reduce costs to make goods more affordable generally. The global economy is now so thoroughly interdependent that whatever you do throughout your day, you are doing it alongside an invisible army of child slaves.

There have emerged three approaches to trying to understand what globalization means for child slavery rights.

First, what can be called a "neoliberal" argument claims that contemporary globalization is in fact reducing child slavery overall. This is because, despite human rights abuses in some sectors of the market, globalization in general is creating more efficient marketplaces that reduce global poverty overall, and global poverty is the primary cause of child slavery in the first place.

While they do not endorse child slavery, organizations such as the International Monetary Fund, the World Bank, and the World Trade Organization tend to view the problem of child slavery as arising out of deep poverty and hence solvable in the long run only through increasingly free world markets. Some in the so-called Global South even claim that "the employment of children is justified in that it is a necessary step in the progress of these developing countries, like it was when the United States and the developed countries of Western Europe were in similar stages of development."[36]

The economist Jagdish Bhagwati argues along such lines that global markets have reduced, rather than increased, both ordinary and exploitative child labor. This is because, in his view, the past few decades of free-market growth have created greater prosperity and access to credit around the world, thus reducing the incentive on parents and communities to put their children to work while simultaneously increasing their incentive to send children to school. He cites the example of 1990s Vietnam, which embraced market reform by reducing export quotas on its primary staple, rice. This raised the price of rice 29 percent to match global prices, resulting in rising incomes for many Vietnamese farmers and corresponding declines in child labor and increases in school attendance.[37]

Second, what can be called a "humanitarian" argument claims, in contrast, that child slavery is not simply an unfortunate by-product of globalization but arises implicitly from it. Global marketplaces will exploit children's labor to create efficiencies unless reined in by the international human rights community.

An example is how multinational corporations hold power over the garment industry in India. According to Nicola Phillips, global companies monopolize resources and prices by means of "large-scale outsourcing and . . . harnessing of an informality-mobility nexus."[38] They pressure national governments to lower regulatory obstacles or at least turn a blind eye to exploitative practices. The result is that garment and other global industries continually shift resources and manufacturing across borders, following the logic of the global marketplace, in order to take maximum advantage of local impoverished conditions.

Global markets run more efficiently, in this view, the more they can exploit the low costs of child labor and the more they can prevent effective child labor regulation.

The solution, in this case, is not less market regulation but more. International labor protections need to be given the same powerful teeth as were previously developed in national ones. An influential international network of activists, NGOs, and human rights groups called the World Social Forum, for example, "stand[s] in opposition to a process of globalization commanded by the large multinational corporations and by the governments and international institutions at the service of those corporations' interests" and works instead "to ensure that globalization in solidarity will prevail as a new stage in world history [that] will respect universal human rights."[39]

This kind of global human rights solidarity involves banning the worst kinds of labor exploitation through international conventions and consciousness raising. It also seeks to remove the underlying conditions of children's extreme poverty through rights to education, health care, and economic security.

Finally, what can be called an "empowerment" argument claims that while the problem lies in neoliberal global markets, the solution does not lie as much in protecting children as in giving them rights to empowerment. A protection approach treats children as victims, in this view, while empowerment gets to the root of the problem and treats children instead as agents and fighters. History shows that slavery is only ultimately defeated when those formerly oppressed by their societies win equal rights to social and political freedoms.

A good example here is the worldwide growth of child and youth labor unions. These operate at various local, national, and international levels. For example, NATs (Niños y Adolescentes Trabajadores) labor unions in Latin America have empowered all ages of children to fight for rights to work without exploitation and with dignity.[40] Such movements sometimes find themselves at odds with international humanitarian pressures from the UN and ILO to ban child labor altogether. And they certainly run up against the global corporations benefitting from child labor. However, children such as shoe industry workers in Brazil have effectively raised consciousness about their situations and improved working conditions and pay.[41]

Matías Cordero Arce argues that child labor movements represent a kind of "cosmopolitanism" or "globalization from below." Children are able to empower themselves through a "cross-border solidarity among groups that are exploited, oppressed, or excluded by hegemonic globalization."[42] On March 9, 2011, the Movements of Working Children and Adolescents of Latin America issued a statement to the United Nations Human Rights Council's session on children's rights demanding that it make a clear distinction between exploitative and legitimate child labor.

Child union representatives participated actively in the 2011 World Social Forum held in Dakar on issues such as child mobility and violence against children at work.[43]

From this perspective, the solution to children's labor exploitation is for children themselves to be empowered to stand up for their own rights, just as, in the past, have women, minorities, and the poor in similar situations. It is for children to gain rights to fight for their rights for themselves.

Each of these approaches tackles the impact of globalization on child slavery in a correspondingly global way. Neoliberalism harnesses global markets to reduce child poverty. Humanitarianism uses global governance to create powerful regulations. And empowerment shapes global interconnections into grassroots anti-exploitation movements. Clearly, new ideas and practices are needed to match new global realities. Perhaps a combination of all three approaches is ultimately required—wherever the emphasis may be placed—to provide child laborers the dignity and conditions they deserve.

HOW CAN CHILD SLAVERY BE ADDRESSED THROUGH LAW?

Ishmael Beah fought as a child soldier in the Sierra Leone civil war of the 1990s. Beah started fighting for the government army at the age of twelve after his village had been destroyed and his family killed by rebels. According to his own account, he had little choice but to join the fighting to save his own life. Government forces trained him in weaponry and got him addicted to drugs that allowed him to stay awake and fight for days and without fear. For two years, Beah participated in countless killings, executions, and destruction of entire villages. He was eventually rescued and rehabilitated by UNICEF, moved to the United States, attended university, wrote a best-selling book about his experiences, and became a member of the Human Rights Watch Children's Rights Division Advisory Council.[44]

Children as young as nine have probably fought in all the major wars of history. According to David Rosen, it was only after World War I that they started to be viewed as victims of exploitation instead of voluntary recruits and even heroes.[45] Children fought on both sides of the American Civil War to much acclaim. They joined combat not only in World Wars I and II but also in the French and other resistance movements against the Nazis. As we have seen, there are an estimated three hundred thousand child soldiers in the world today. Despite international condemnation, they are fighting in approximately twenty countries, including in the Palestinian liberation movement, Middle Eastern terrorism, and armed conflicts in Chechnya, Afghanistan, Syria, and the Democratic Republic of Congo.

Child soldiering illustrates the conundrums involved in addressing child slavery through law. Here are just five central difficulties.

First, international law is not entirely clear about minimum legal ages.

The ILO's 1999 Convention No. 182 (on the worst forms of child labor) did in fact raise the minimum age in which a person can legally participate in armed conflict to eighteen. Prior to that, the ILO antislavery conventions, the Geneva Conventions, and even the CRC only banned the use and recruitment of child soldiers under the age of fifteen.

But the International Criminal Court's (ICC's) Rome Statute of 1998 (article 8.2.b.xxvi) still only makes it a war crime to conscript, enlist, or use in hostilities children under fifteen. And the 2002 CRC Optional Protocol on the involvement of children in armed conflict, while raising the age to eighteen at which soldiers can "take a direct part in hostilities" (article 1) or be "compulsorily recruited" (article 2), still permits "voluntary recruitment" as young as fifteen (article 3). As Claire Breen has noted, states still enjoy wide legal latitude to ignore a "straight 18" ban on child soldiering.[46]

A second issue is that it is not always clear what is meant, legally, by "voluntary" recruitment.

For example, some groups have argued that the US government's Junior Reserve Officer Training Corps (JROTC) program violates international law by effectively operating as a recruitment program for children as young as fourteen. While the official aim of the JROTC is "to instill in students in secondary educational institutions the values of citizenship, service to the United States, and personal responsibility and a sense of accomplishment," in fact US Army documents laud it as a highly effective tool to "facilitate recruiter access to cadets in JROTC program and to the entire student body."[47] There are currently over three thousand JROTC units with over five hundred thousand cadets in high schools across the United States, largely in poorer districts, and 30–50 percent of JROTC members eventually go on to serve in the US military.[48]

JROTC has been criticized as "voluntary" only in a narrow sense. First of all, recruits are not on the whole made explicitly aware of the program's hidden recruitment aims. Second, teenagers targeted by JROTC often lack other viable educational and economic opportunities. Their schools may otherwise be so poor that they are left with little other choice of activities. Third, students are sometimes enrolled against their will. According to reports in Los Angeles, for example, "high school administrators were enrolling reluctant students in JROTC as an alternative to overcrowded gym classes."[49] And fourth, students are sometimes pressured into joining. Schools may need to keep up minimum enrollments. As a 2006 self-study by the US government found, because of the need for recruits during the Afghanistan and Iraq Wars, JROTC programs sometimes pushed teenagers to join through "overly aggressive tactics, such as coercion and harass-ment," false promises, or failure to obtain parental consent.[50]

Third, it remains a legal question what exactly constitutes chil-dren's "direct combat."

The ICC defines direct combat broadly as any "active partici-pation in hostilities," including not only actual combat but also a broad range of support activities such as scouting, spying, being a decoy or courier, running a checkpoint, guarding military quar-ters or commanders, and providing logistical support such as car-rying loads, acquiring food, and making trails.[51] Not all of these activities involve children's risk of actually becoming engaged in fighting. But, arguably, they do all fit the broader definition of child slavery, that is, labor that is exploitative or hazardous. Should all such activities be banned as violations of children's rights, or only the most dangerous ones?

Fourth, the vast majority of child soldiers in twenty-first-centu-ry conflicts are fighting not for national armies but for nonstate actors such as rebel or terrorist organizations that are not signato-ries to international conventions. Is it technically illegal for such organizations to employ child soldiers if they did not agree to ILO and UN conventions banning child soldiering in the first place?

This problem helped to motivate the 2007 Paris Commit-ments, a nonbinding agreement between fifty-nine countries that pledges, in part, "to prevent armed groups within the jurisdiction of our State that are distinct from our armed forces from recruit-ing or using children under 18 years of age in hostilities" (article 4). Children's rights against fighting are to be protected through monitoring, investigating, and prosecuting groups that use child soldiers; treating such children primarily as victims rather than perpetrators of crimes; and providing asylum for refugee children escaping war zones in other countries.[52] But on the whole, rebel and terrorist groups themselves have little reason to follow international laws created by the very states they are generally fighting against.

The one tool that has proved effective against nonstate actors, though only partially so, is the above-mentioned Rome Statute, which allows for the creation of special international courts to try violators of international norms. Special courts have been established to prosecute the recruitment and use of child soldiers in East Timor, Sierra Leone, and Iraq. For example, of the twenty-two people so far indicted by the Special Court for Sierra Leone (SCSL), seven were convicted of recruiting and using child soldiers. Similarly, the first person ever convicted by the International Criminal Court (ICC), established to prosecute the Rome Statute worldwide, was Thomas Lubanga Dyilo, a rebel leader in the Democratic Republic of Congo who was found guilty in 2012 of enlisting, conscripting, and using child soldiers, for which he was ultimately sentenced to fourteen years in prison.[53]

Fifth and finally, there is debate about whether child soldiers themselves should be liable to prosecution for war crimes.

There is international legal precedent for holding child soldiers criminally responsible. Children were tried for war crimes committed during World War II. The Geneva Conventions Optional Protocol I, article 77, assumes child liability by prohibiting arrested children from being given the death penalty. The Paris Commitments' article 11 states that children under eighteen who have served in armed forces "should be treated in accordance with international standards for juvenile justice."

While the ICC is forbidden by the Rome Statutes from trying anyone under eighteen, other regional courts such as the Sierra Leone Special Court tried minors as young as fifteen and the East Timor Special Panels as young as twelve. Since 2000, the government of the Democratic Republic of Congo has executed one fourteen-year-old child soldier for war crimes and sentenced twenty others to death. In Rwanda, minors have been tried and sentenced for genocide. Several children worldwide have been denied asylum status for participating in armed conflict or terrorism.[54] In 2002–2003, the United States detained at least fifteen (and potentially twenty-one if exact ages were known) children under eighteen at the Guantanamo Bay detention camp, two of them initially aged thirteen, though none have so far been put on trial.[55]

The legal scholar Joseph Rikhof argues that while there is international consensus that immunity should be granted to all children under twelve, from ages twelve through seventeen it should be permissible to try children for war crimes under certain conditions. These conditions should be stricter than those for adults. The first is to set a high bar for the child's *mens rea*, or mental culpability: specifically, that the child did not act under mental illness, intoxication, or duress. A child soldier could potentially be cleared, for example, if he or she were forced into a drug addiction or threatened with violence. Second, it would also have to be proved that the child soldier had the "intention" to commit war crimes or crimes against humanity and "knew" that his or her acts were such crimes. Third and finally, the crime should be limited to acts that the international community agrees constitute acts of hostility—for example, direct combat but not food gathering.[56] While some might argue, then, that no persons under eighteen should be held criminally liable for war crimes, it can also be argued that within limits they should.

These legal conundrums about child soldiering help to illustrate many of the legal issues surrounding child slavery in general.

Below what age should exploitative or hazardous labor not be tolerated at all? Can a child's entry into exploitative labor ever be defined as legally voluntary? What is the exact line between a minor's nonforced and forced labor? To what legal standards can states and the international community hold nonstate actors? When, if at all, should children themselves working in slave-like conditions such as war, prostitution, and drug smuggling be held legally accountable for their own criminal behavior?

WHAT ABOUT HUMAN RIGHTS MORE BROADLY?

Sumathi is one of more than 325,000 children who work in the beedi (hand-rolled cigarette) industry in the southern state of Tamil Nadu in India. She was bonded to a beedi agent at the age of seven, meaning that her family agreed that she would work for him in exchange for her family receiving a loan of one thousand rupees (approximately fifteen US dollars), to be paid back at 300–500 percent annual interest. Five years later, Sumathi, now twelve, earns five rupees (eight US cents) a day rolling 1,500 beedis for ten to fourteen hours, which is approximately 25 percent of the wages she would earn on the open market. Her two younger sisters, aged eight and nine, have also become bonded for one thousand rupees each and work similar hours alongside Sumathi as tip closers, earning three rupees (five cents) a day.

Sumathi reports that "my father and mother force me to go work with the agent . . . [and] every week the agent gives my wages to my parents. If it is less money than usual, they beat me." Beedi rolling can result in chronic back pain, repetitive wrist and hand injuries, and lung disease from inhaling tobacco dust.[57] On the other hand, much like families in the United States who become trapped in cycles of "payday loan" debts, Sumathi and her family live in such unbreakable poverty that they have few other choices than to take on these kinds of bonds.

In terms of Sumathi's legal rights, India outlawed hazardous labor for children below the age of fourteen in its 1986 Child Labour (Prohibition and Regulation) Act. The result of this act, however, was to drive most hazardous child labor underground, moving from the visible world of factories to the invisible world of private households. Indeed, the Child Labor Act does not prohibit hazardous labor within the home. As a result, many children like Sumathi and her sisters still work long hours in exploitative labor for local and global corporations, but now beyond the eyes of the law.

Sumathi's situation highlights the fact that child slavery needs to be addressed not only as a matter of law but also as a matter of broader human rights.

A human rights approach would require, first and foremost, clarity about the nature of the problem.

As we have seen, children end up in exploitative labor for complex and often conflicting reasons. Child slavery is usually some combination of forced and chosen. Sumathi is forced by her circumstances but also chose to work to help her family survive.

For many children and families around the world, the options are stark and exploitation is preferable to starvation. As a mother in Belabadan, India, puts it, "To fill our stomachs, we have to work; whether it is the old or the young."[58] In such cases, the UN, NGOs, or the government simply swooping in to protect children from slave-like labor can end up being even more harmful to children's rights than the labor itself. Children also have rights to life, survival, and economic security, not to mention rights to make choices for themselves under difficult circumstances.

Even without the threat of immediate starvation, some children choose exploitative labor for potential benefits in the future. A study of Muslim girl domestic servants in India, for example, concludes that in most cases, despite the girls working long hours for little pay and despite all the hazards involved, "mothers put their children to work not, we suggest, for the immediate benefits of the work (i.e., the wages) but because these contacts form part of a web of support that poor working-class households need to assemble so as to be able to survive economic shocks and maintain inter-class/caste social networks that make them people worth bothering about."[59] That is, exploitative labor can be seen by children and families as a means to a larger end, a necessary evil for creating a more sustainable future.

And then there are issues of cultural interpretation. For example, some girls in Karnataka, India, choose (in some sense) to work as *devadasis*, or religious sex workers, as part of their cultural heritage. Interviews show in part that "they do not reveal themselves to be the frightened, brainwashed victims of parental or systemic violence depicted in most accounts of child prostitution. Instead, they present themselves as girls who may not always like what they do or what is demanded of them, but do so out of a sense of filial duty, economic need, and because doing *dhandha* [sex work] is incorporated into their models of female maturity."[60] Being a *devadasi* may be an important rite of cultural passage. Similar arguments are made about boy soldiers sometimes making particular cultural transitions into manhood.

Another way to look at this basic human rights issue is to ask how rights to protection against exploitative labor can be balanced with other kinds of rights to the provision of resources and participation in choices.[61] In general, we have seen throughout this book that the boundaries between these three different kinds of rights are porous at best. Their various ambitions need to be constantly balanced against each other.

For example, protection rights against children's labor exploitation are closely intertwined with provision rights to an education. The largest NGO in India currently working for children's education, Pratham, does so for the specific purpose of reducing child labor.[62] Similarly, the MV Foundation, a local NGO in Hyderabad, India, turned its attention from directly fighting child labor to improving schools, registering children for school, and educating parents about the value of schooling—all in an attempt to make not working a realistic option.[63] As Eric Edmonds and Nina Pavcnik argue, "If a more rapid reduction in the general incidence of child labor is a policy goal, improving educational systems and providing financial incentives to poor families to send children to school may be more useful solutions to the child labor problem than punitive measures designed to prevent children from earning income."[64]

At the same time, protections against slave-like labor have to be balanced against children's rights to choices and empowerment. It would be self-contradictory to remove children from forced labor without considering their own views and desires in the matter. Just as with slavery in the past, eradicating child slavery today must include a combination of both top-down protections and provisions with bottom-up economic and cultural means of empowerment.

For example, Anti-Slavery International argues that child slaves need to be provided with spaces, workshops, and other environments from which "to break out of their isolation and interact with others" and "to seek their rights to just wages, holidays, and time off to go to classes." This kind of organizational infrastructure can include child labor unions that demand labor rights, NGOs that raise awareness, and community groups that identify laboring children and offer them safe spaces to assemble. It can also mean including present and former child slaves in developing internationally recognized "good practices" that demand, for example, "that [child laborers] should be regularly and meaningfully consulted; that they should be helped to organise their own activities; and that they should take part in advocacy."[65]

These kinds of grassroots children's rights approaches are cropping up in local communities around the world. An organization in Delhi, India, called Childhood Enhancement through Training and Action (CHETNA) helps working street children form their own groups to support one another, report violations, and lobby for their rights.[66] Another initiative in Delhi is the Child Workers Union (Bal Mazdoor) organized by the local children's council. As Beeru, a fourteen-year-old rag picker in the union, reports: "We have come to understand the importance of our unity which is our biggest asset, our strength in front of which no-one can stand. . . . [I]t is our unity that will help us in defeating our exploiters."[67]

These are but two examples of what Arjun Appadurai calls "globalization from below," that is, grassroots movements working to counteract the injustices of "globalization from above" by organizing marginalized groups like child laborers to fight for their rights for themselves.[68]

It makes sense that children who are capable of factory work, farming, domestic servitude, prostitution, soldiering, and many other forms of labor should also be capable of organizing and advocating for themselves. It is too simple to view child laborers, however deeply exploited, as merely passive victims of adults. It is children's very capacities for agency and participation that are being exploited in the first place.

This does not mean that labor exploitation is something that people can simply oppose by themselves. Children are imprisoned in exploitative labor by violence, threats, debt bondage, or lack of realistic alternatives. Just like adults, they depend for assistance on others around them, whether family, local communities, NGOs, national governments, or more just international marketplaces. But again like adults, this does not mean that children do not have rights to participate in the means by which their conditions can be addressed.

CONCLUSION

From the broadest perspective, child slavery is an issue of child empowerment. Put differently, it is one particularly egregious form of human disempowerment. It is forced upon individuals by a diverse web of family and local conditions, economic realities, government and legal inaction, and globalized marketplaces. To become empowered under such circumstances is thus equally multilayered. It means gaining human rights all at once to protections against harm and exploitation, provisions of economic and educational opportunities, and participation in influencing one's environment.

Whether in domestic servitude, industrial labor, agriculture, street work, sex work, soldiering, or any other area, children's labor exploitation is bound up with the second-class citizenship of children in the human rights community overall. Responses to child slavery have to include respect for the dignity of children as children. The idea of "the human" has to include children as fully as adults. It has to recognize that all humans are vulnerable to great exploitation as well as capable of great agency.

And this means, again, broadening our understanding of human rights themselves. The Enlightenment idea of rights did not deal well with slavery at the time, and it deals even more poorly with globalized slavery today. Rights can no longer adequately be understood simply as individual freedoms. Such a view cannot tell the difference between the freedoms of a global corporation and the freedoms of a child in poverty. Rights need instead to be understood as means of social empowerment and inclusion. Child slaves may have choices, but they can make choices only within exceptionally limited circumstances created by larger webs of relationship with others.

My breakfast this morning resulted from a vast interdependent network of economic relationships without which I could not survive. If a nine-year-old in California found herself spending all day harvesting the sugar for my cereal, she too is only trying to survive and thrive in this world. The only difference is that she can do so only under larger exploitative conditions. Child slavery ultimately violates the right for each and every one of us to be empowered members of our local and global economies.

6

THE RIGHT TO VOTE

The final case study we take up is children's rights to vote.

The challenge here is different than in the previous two chapters. It is less one of understanding or implementation than of considering new and controversial possibilities. For it is almost completely unheard of in history for children and youth to be considered eligible to vote. Few other rights more clearly separate the adult from the child. What is more, voting rights are fundamental. They are perhaps the most important right of citizenship. They are rights to determine one's society's very rights, to elect representatives who will make the very laws and policies under which everyone must live.

Nevertheless, while the challenge of children voting remains largely theoretical, there are in fact children, scholars, activists, and policymakers who are starting to consider it. The debate is very much in its infancy, somewhat where the women's suffrage movement stood a century and a half ago. Even the idea of children voting is controversial. Many who study and advocate for children's rights would oppose extending these rights to include voting. But whatever one's views, voting rights are a useful test case—perhaps the ultimate test case—for thinking about children's rights at their most basic level.

This chapter is a challenge in another way too. So far I have largely kept my own views in the background. True, I have suggested a particular theoretical framework that I call childism. I have also made a few arguments in favor of particular children's rights practices. But in this chapter, I will explain my own thinking in detail. I have spent significant time writing about this question and my beliefs have evolved over the years.[1] I will make every effort to be fair in comparing my own views with those of others. My aim here is less to convince you than to challenge you to consider the question carefully.

What I have come to believe is that all persons, child and adult alike, should have the right to vote. But at the same time, this right to vote needs to be understood and exercised differently. In line with childism, voting should not simply be extended to children on adult terms but rather rethought for both children and adults to include children as children. What I ultimately argue for is a "proxy-claim" right to vote for all. By this I mean that all citizens at birth should be given a vote that is initially used by their closest proxy, such as a parent or a guardian. Then they should be able to claim their vote whenever they wish to exercise it for themselves. A proxy-claim vote is the best way, I contend, to include the entire *demos* or people, instead of just adults, as equal members of a democracy.

Voting can be taken as an example of children's larger participation rights, rights, that is, to exercise agency and voice in public life.

Other such rights are numerous. They include political rights such as free speech, political organization, and citizenship; civil rights such as taking part in associations, influencing schooling and education, and having opportunities for leisure and play; economic rights such as freedom of work, ownership of property, and access to consumer products; cultural rights such as the free exercise of religion and access to media and information; judicial rights such as self-representation in court and suing for damages; and social rights such as having an abortion, making medical decisions, and expressing one's sexual orientation.

In general, children's participation rights are more controversial than other kinds of children's rights. They move children decisively from objects of adult saving to subjects of self-empowerment. Many people believe that participation rights make children too much like adults. Others believe they are too individualistic and Western. And often, as especially in the case of voting, they directly challenge the authority of adults. But it is precisely these kinds of controversies that help us think about children's rights more critically and creatively.

In terms of voting, we will proceed, as in previous chapters, by asking basic questions. Why have children historically been denied the right to vote? Are children sufficiently competent, knowledgeable, and independent to vote? Would children's voting cause harm to children themselves, adults, or society? Would children's suffrage require a new theoretical basis for suffrage itself? Would child-inclusive voting work in reality?

WHY HAVE CHILDREN BEEN DENIED THE RIGHT TO VOTE?

The first question is a historical one. While it may seem obvious for children not to vote, this idea is based on a history of beliefs about voting that evolved over time.

The first thing that history tells us is that the right to vote has grown dramatically. The idea of a universal adult vote is extremely recent. Women only began to vote within the past century and gained the vote in *all* democracies only in 2015. It was only in 1969 that the voting age was first reduced from twenty-one to eighteen. Up until less than two hundred years ago, voting was a right only for a very small number of wealthy white adult males.

This exponential rise in voting rights can be seen through the story of six major voting landmarks.

1. *Nobility and clergy.* Apart from a few restricted instances in ancient Greece, India, and Rome, lasting voting rights were first established soon after 1066 in Norman England, when William the Conqueror granted members of the nobility and clergy the right to elect a Great Council to approve the laws of the Crown. This Great Council eventually drafted the 1215 Magna Carta that forced King John to accept substantial nobility oversight. It evolved shortly thereafter into the first so-called parliament, whose name is derived from the Latin for discussion or speech.

2. *Householding white males.* About fifty years later, in 1265, this same parliament in England extended the vote to all free male householders, that is, the small minority of men who actually owned land. A century and a half after that, in 1430, this right was then cut back to only "forty shilling freeholders," or householding males who earned at least forty shillings in annual rent from their properties. It was not until the United States' 1777 Articles of Confederation and 1789 Constitution that the broader vote from 1265 of all property-owning white adult males was reinstituted.

3. *Non-property-owning white adult males.* It took almost six hundred years after householding males first gained the vote for it to begin to be extended to non-property-owning white men, in the first instance through the United States' Fourteenth Amendment of 1828. The United Kingdom's Reform Acts of 1832 and 1867 subsequently also extended suffrage to adult male renters; and its Representation of the People Acts of 1884 and 1918 further extended voting rights to all adult males twenty-one and over regardless of property qualifications.

4. *Minority adult males.* The first nonwhite men ever to be enfranchised were the Maori in New Zealand in 1865 following the Maori War. The US Constitution's 1870 Fifteenth Amend-

ment similarly extended the vote to adult males regardless of race, color, or previous servitude (though it was not until the 1964 Twenty-Fifth Amendment that US minorities could vote regardless of failure to pay poll or other types of racially based taxes). Other examples of minorities receiving the right to vote were Jews in Romania in 1923 and blacks and coloreds in South Africa upon the end of apartheid in 1994.

5. *Women*. The first national rights of women to vote were granted in New Zealand in 1893. These were followed by Australia in 1902, Finland in 1906 (when women were also granted the first ever rights to run for elected office), Canada in 1917, and Poland in 1918. (There were select instances of women voting prior to these dates in local elections.) Women gained national suffrage in the United States through the Nineteenth Amendment in 1920 and in the UK through the Representation of the People Act of 1928. Women's suffrage took over a century to become fully universal. It was granted, for example, in Turkey in 1930, Japan in 1947, India in 1950, Iran in 1963, Nigeria in 1978, Qatar in 1999, the United Arab Emirates in 2006, and the very last country, Saudi Arabia, in 2015.

6. *Eighteen-year-olds*. The voting age was lowered for the first time from twenty-one to eighteen in Czechoslovakia in 1946, followed by sixteen other countries over the next two decades. The first Western European country to lower the age to eighteen was the United Kingdom, through its Representation of the People Act of 1969. The US voting age was lowered to eighteen through the Twenty-Sixth Amendment of 1971.[2] India, Switzerland, Austria, and Morocco lowered the voting age to eighteen around the turn of the twenty-first century, and Japan in 2016. The voting age is still twenty-one in ten countries and twenty in three more.

What does this very brief historical sketch tell us? It tells us that the right to vote is not fixed in stone. It has changed dramatically over time. Even a universal adult vote is very recent (indeed still not entirely complete). A thousand years ago, only a tiny minority was empowered to vote. By far the vast majority of adults gained suffrage just within the past hundred years. What is more, the adult vote remains largely only symbolic in less-than-democratic countries like China, Iran, and North Korea. And even in full democracies, large segments of the adult population do not have the right to vote, such as noncitizens and sometimes felons. For example, 5.9 million (or 2.5 percent) of adult Americans do not have the right to vote because they are in prison or have felony convictions. On top of all this, of course, are the problems of money and corruption, which dilute the real effectiveness and meaning of the right to vote, often significantly.

What this history also suggests is that there has been a radical shift over time in what voting actually means. For voting is a very different idea when it is no longer just a privilege of the nobility but also landowners representing their tenants. Or when it shifts from a power of landed gentry to one for all male heads of households to represent their families. Or when it is required to include all men in their racial and ethnic diversity. Or when the gender barrier is broken and voters are not just heads of households but all adults as individuals.

The very theoretical bases of voting have continually transformed over time and can continue to transform in the future.

WHAT ABOUT CHILDREN?

This history also tells us that the one group that has persistently been denied the right to vote is the third of humanity who are under the age of eighteen. This is so much the case that policymakers regularly use the term "universal suffrage" to refer to voting rights only for adult men and women.

This unstated assumption is found, for example, in article 21 of the founding charter of the United Nations, the 1948 Declaration of Human Rights, in which all signatory countries pledge themselves to "universal and equal suffrage," even though none at the time considered that to mean anyone under twenty-one.

But the situation is starting to change.

One kind of change, albeit rather indirect: many local and national governments now have systematic ways of listening to children's political voices. These efforts largely follow the CRC's call in article 12 for children's "right to express [their] views freely in all matters affecting the child." Of course, it has always been an option for representatives to listen to children. But increasingly governments are turning this option from an adult prerogative into a children's right.

For example, in 2001 New Zealand initiated its Agenda for Children, which is a regular forum for the government to consult children and youth on national issues.[3] In 2003, South Africa launched the Children in Action (Dikwankwetla) project, in which children are given the opportunity to address parliamentary hearings on children's issues.[4] In 2004, the United Kingdom appointed four Children's Commissioners (one each for England, Scotland, Wales, and Northern Ireland) to represent children's views in legislation and policy.[5] The Israeli Knesset regularly invites children to participate in its child-related committees.[6] In 2009, the Kazakhstan government worked with UNICEF to organize a National Adolescents and Youth Forum, an annual political consultative process with youth aged ten to twenty-four.[7]

Of course, these initiatives fall far short of children's right to vote. But they do recognize children's rights to some level of direct political voice and representation. They are a step beyond the traditional view that adults already know what children require politically without having to ask them.

Second, and more directly, many countries now have children's parliaments. We already met Tazim Ali at the outset of this book, the nine-year-old president of the children's parliament of

Varanasi, India. Since the 1990s, approximately thirty countries
have developed national children's parliaments, that is, parallel
parliamentary systems for children and youth that mirror those
for adults. These countries include India (where the first were
created in 1994 in the state of Rajasthan), Sri Lanka, Norway,
Finland, Germany, Slovenia, Bolivia, Ecuador, Brazil, Nigeria,
Zimbabwe, Congo, Burkina Faso, Liberia, New Zealand, Scotland, and a Children's United Parliament of the World.[8]

Children's parliaments generally operate from the village or
school level up to district and then national levels. Children elect
local representatives, who in turn vote for regional representatives, and so on. Often there are two separate parliaments: a
house for younger children around five to eleven and a senate for
adolescents twelve to seventeen.

Children's parliaments have been criticized for often being
merely tokenistic or educational, that is, listening to children
without allowing them influence or merely training children for
adulthood. They have also been criticized for favoring already
privileged groups of children.[9]

But many children's parliaments have in fact been organized in
such a way as to actually influence public policy.[10] For example,
the children's parliament of the city of Barra Mansa in Brazil
partially controls government budgets having to do with schools
and recreation.[11] Local children's parliaments in India have
brought new services to communities such as clean water, working sewage systems, and streetlights. The younger children's parliament of Bolivia regularly pressures the adult parliament to address issues such as child abuse, discrimination against disabled
children, unequal educational resources for indigenous children,
and the lack of career opportunities for working children and
parents.[12]

Of course, separate children's parliaments are still not quite
the same as the right to vote. Indeed, they can provide window

dressing that obscures children's actual lack of power. This is why women, for example, did not ultimately press in the past for separate women's parliaments. Nevertheless, children's parliaments do demonstrate that even quite young children, if given the chance, can participate in serious public debate and vote on important political issues.

Finally, at least thirteen countries and many more cities have now lowered the voting age to sixteen. These countries include Brazil—the first to do so, in 1988—Argentina, Austria, Bosnia and Herzegovina, Croatia, Cuba, Dominican Republic, Ecuador, Hungary, Indonesia, Nicaragua, Serbia, and Slovenia, as well as select regions such as the British Channel Islands and parts of Norway. Two US cities recently lowered the local voting age to sixteen: Takoma Park and Hyattsville, both in Maryland. Germany and Israel permit votes at sixteen in local elections. Other countries have voting ages of seventeen, including East Timor, Indonesia, Seychelles, Sudan, and some states in the US for primary elections if the person will turn eighteen by the time of the general election. [13]

The UK Labour Party, partly in response to pressure from youth groups, tried but failed to lower the voting age to sixteen in 2004 and still has "Votes at Sixteen" in its official party platform. [14] In the United States, a youth-run organization called the National Youth Rights Association has pressed for several years to lower the voting age to sixteen and even helped to introduce a (defeated) bill in California in 2004 to permit a one-quarter vote at fourteen and a one-half vote at sixteen. [15]

The most radical step to date is a bill in the German national parliament that was proposed in 2008 but never voted on. The bill was initiated by organizations such as the child-run policy group KRÄTZÄ and the Family Party of Germany and was sponsored by a multiparty group of forty-six liberal and conservative parliamentarians. The proposal was for a constitutional amendment to grant a proxy vote to all German citizens at birth that would be exercised by parents or guardians until they believe the child is ready to use it.[16] This idea is similar to the one I will propose, except that I believe it is the children and not the parents who should decide when to claim the vote for themselves.

These efforts toward children's suffrage are piecemeal and almost invisible to public consciousness. Nevertheless, compared to the history of suffrage outlined above, they are genuinely new and real developments. Interestingly, unlike in previous suffrage movements, children's suffrage is primarily being championed first in poorer countries, where, perhaps, children tend to be more integrated into public life through work and labor unions. It was likewise labor unions that arguably succeeded in first pressing for suffrage for women.[17] But children and child advocates are now organizing worldwide and beginning to form what could be called an embryonic child suffrage movement.

ARE CHILDREN SUFFICIENTLY COMPETENT?

The most frequently debated question concerning whether children should have rights to vote is whether children possess the requisite competency. Are children sufficiently capable of public thought, democratic debate, weighing consequences, and assuming the responsibilities of exercising real political power?

Some argue that common sense and developmental psychology say no.

The philosopher David Archard has developed this argument more fully than anyone else. He concludes that minors lack the competence for voting because "we do not know what a child would choose if possessed of adult rational powers of choice because what makes a child a child is just her lack of such powers (her ignorance, inconstant wants, inconsistent beliefs and limited powers of ratiocination)."[18] Childhood is the time in life during which political competencies are still developing. No one comes into the world with fully formed political skills. It takes time and education to choose, for example, whether leaders should take a country to war. As Benjamin Barber has put it slightly differently, children have still not developed the core political skill of "civility": the ability to deliberate publicly in a productive and reciprocal way.[19]

Influential political theorists agree. John Rawls, the most significant American political philosopher of the late twentieth century, assumes that voting is only for adults. Only adults can think with the requisite democratic "universality" and "impartiality."[20] More recently, the major German political theorist Jürgen Habermas uses moral psychology to argue that children lack the full "communicative competence" needed to engage in genuine social and political "reciprocal perspective taking."[21] If democratic life is about public argumentation, then it requires capacities for understanding others and trying to reach consensus, capacities that take time and experience to develop.

Developmental psychologists themselves have also weighed in on this question. Interestingly, Daniel Hart and Robert Atkins conclude from a survey of 4,217 American adolescents between fourteen and eighteen years of age that, in fact, "16- and 17-year-olds meet minimal criteria for full citizenship and can vote responsibly,"[22] while fourteen- and fifteen-year-olds still lack sufficient competences in political skill, tolerance, and civic knowledge. Starting at age sixteen, however, these capacities plateau at the same level at which they will remain throughout adulthood, and "there is no neurological evidence that indicates that 16- and 17-year-olds lack the requisite neurological maturation necessary for citizenship or for responsible voting."[23]

There are three main difficulties with these competency arguments, however.

First, it is not clear that competence should in fact be a requirement for the right to vote.

No adult has to prove his or her competence in order to enjoy suffrage. Indeed, many adults demonstrably lack capacities for deliberation, reciprocity, discourse, and civility. Few adults, for example, score highly on Habermas's test of "reciprocal perspective taking," a test taken from Lawrence Kohlberg's now widely discredited claim that such skills develop in a single and culturally universal pattern. The competence argument has historically been used to deny voting rights to the poor, minorities, and women. If it also to be used against children, it should be much more persuasively explicated.

Competence should at least not be used as a double standard: applied to children but not to adults. As Bob Franklin has argued concerning children voting, "The presence or absence of rationality does not justify the exclusion of children from political rights but the exclusion, if anyone, of the irrational."[24] If a particular level of competence were indeed a legal requirement for suffrage, then one could argue that many schizophrenic, senile, low IQ, or even just thoughtless adults should be denied it, while many intelligent, politically active, or even just ordinary children and youth should not. As Francis Schrag puts it, any imposition of a competence requirement for child suffrage "might be used to limit *adult* suffrage or to grant some adults more votes than others."[25]

Second, even were competence established as a voting requirement, it should be defined broadly and inclusively rather than narrowly.

The purpose of democratic voting, after all, is to hold representatives accountable to the will of the entire people. We have seen that children as young as five are in fact capable of making important political choices, such as voting in children's parliaments, debating political issues, and representing the views of other children and adults.

Along these lines, Claudio López-Guerra argues, in a lengthy discussion of who should have the right to vote, that children should be included because they are capable of exercising what he calls "the franchise capacity." This he defines as "the faculties to understand and value the act of voting—what an election is about, what the options stand for, and so on."[26] Even if children cannot, say, always make significant medical decisions for themselves, or still have much to learn in school, most can understand what it means to vote. From this point of view, "justice would be best served by abolishing all requirements for voting based on age and mental aptitude."[27]

To be truly democratic, the competence to vote ought to be defined as a basic minimum rather than as a developmental maximum. The broadest meaningful definition would be the capacity to understand voting's basic meaning and purpose. This includes such things as comprehending democratic values, being able to make political choices, and having the ability to express one's own views. These are unfortunately not clear-cut competencies. One could argue that many adults lack them. But voting competencies should be understood broadly rather than narrowly so as to be as democratic as possible.

In my view, an inclusive perspective makes it clear that voting competence does not suddenly spring into being at the age of eighteen or even sixteen. Much younger people have already proved themselves entirely competent and eager to participate in serious political action. The developmental psychologist Charles Helwig has shown that, contrary to the Piagetian developmental model, "even very young children (beginning around three years of age) distinguish moral rules, based on justice and concern for others' welfare, from social conventional rules and customs."[28] More broadly, very young children around the world demonstrate all manner of competencies to work, represent their families, organize politically, and so on.

Third and finally, the fact that children have never had the chance to vote means that children's voting competencies remain unknown and certainly underestimated.

If children in fact had the right to vote, they would certainly demonstrate greater political capacity than they currently appear to have. Prior to women's suffrage, most men as well as women assumed that men were significantly more competent to vote. Indeed, with men having greater opportunities to exercise political agency, this may even at the time have been the case empirically. Women never expecting to vote are less likely to develop the voting capacities they actually own. Once given the right to vote, women immediately demonstrated the competency argument's circularity. Men had only appeared more competent to vote because only men had ever been able to exercise voting competency in the first place.

My conclusion is that there may indeed exist a minimum level of competence needed for the right to vote, but this level of competence should be defined broadly and not simply by age. The proper competence required to vote is the capacity to understand voting's meaning and purpose, a capacity demonstrated by the desire for the right to vote for oneself. Any minimum that is more restrictive is discriminating and undemocratic.

ARE CHILDREN SUFFICIENTLY KNOWLEDGEABLE?

Closely related to competence is the question of knowledge. It is possible that children could be basically competent to vote without yet having gained sufficient knowledge of the political options and consequences. That is, they might not yet be able to use the vote in an informed and responsible way.

Many have argued that the knowledge required to vote is something gained over time through education and experience. A well-functioning democracy depends on a well-educated citizenry. Tak Wing Chan and Matthew Clayton argue, for example, that minors should not have the right to vote because they have not acquired sufficient "knowledge of the political system, and understanding of the nature and significance of issues that are the subject of public and political debate."[29]

This view was taken by the UK Electoral Commission in 2004 when it rejected a proposal to lower the voting age to sixteen, claiming that only eighteen-year-olds have acquired "the development of sufficient social awareness."[30] To vote in an informed way involves a number of different kinds of knowledge: how democratic systems function, what constitutes the various branches of government, the alternatives presented by specific political parties, the likely impact of policies on diverse populations, consequences for foreign policy, and so on.

One can, in part, make similar counterarguments here as with competence. If adults do not have to demonstrate a certain level of knowledge to vote, children should not be subject to the double standard of having to do so either. Likewise, children around the world have in fact shown high levels of knowledge of politics, not only in children's parliaments but also in children's involvement in any number of important political causes. Finally, young people may look like they have little voting knowledge, but were they actually permitted to vote, they would certainly gain more knowledge than they currently do.

But banning children from voting because of insufficient knowledge is tricky in other ways too.

First, knowledge requirements are in a sense inherently undemocratic. Jim Crow laws in the American South used knowledge tests to disenfranchise African Americans. Knowledge requirements are inevitably set by those already in power. They cannot easily be inoculated against political bias. Prejudging what counts as voting knowledge undermines a central purpose of voting, which is to force those in power to respond to the maximum possible diversity of knowledge from the population.

Second, even the most basic kind of knowledge required is difficult to determine. Voting could not demand, for example, basic literacy. Many democracies throughout Africa, Asia, and South America, including the world's largest democracy, India, have significant and in some cases mainly illiterate populations. Here, ballots use candidate photos. Nor is it necessary to understand all the political options. The positions of parties and candidates are constantly shifting and open to diverse interpretation. Political knowledge is not an exact science, making it difficult to say with confidence that children and youth by definition do not have it.

Third and most important, even very young children do in fact have political knowledge that, while not always the same as that of adults, is just as important to have heard in public affairs. Men and women, the poor and the wealthy, minorities and majorities share some knowledge of political life and bring to the table some distinctive knowledge of their own. The same is true for adults and children.

Take, for example, issues of war and poverty. Children do experience war, both as its victims and as its perpetrators. Many children around the world have a great deal more knowledge of the realities and consequences of war than I do as an adult who has never experienced it directly. Likewise, children bring significant knowledge about poverty, being disproportionately among the poor. Their ideas about its consequences for them and about potential solutions should be welcomed into political life. Indeed, were politicians directly accountable to the votes of children, they would be forced to understand issues like poverty and war in greater depth.

While it is true, then, that knowledge is important for democracy, this does not mean that children should be barred from voting; on the contrary, it means that their different and diverse perspectives should be welcomed. Political knowledge is not, as assumed in the Enlightenment, a set of universal facts best understood by white, educated gentlemen. Rather, as argued by postcolonialist and postmodernist theorists, political knowledge is the expression of an irreducible diversity of experiences. Democracy works better the more disparate kinds of knowledge and experience it includes. Since children are the group most likely to have their experiences ignored, they are also the group most in need of mechanisms like voting to make their perspectives and experiences heard.

ARE CHILDREN SUFFICIENTLY INDEPENDENT?

A third area of debate, also related to competence and knowledge, is whether children and youth possess sufficient political independence to truly vote for their own interests instead of being manipulated by adults.

Some argue that what is distinct about children is their particular state of dependence. They depend on parents for survival and nurturance, on teachers for learning, on role models and religious leaders for moral development, and so on. As a result, children are uniquely susceptible to political manipulation, whether by immediate adults in their families and neighborhoods or by popular figures in mass media and culture. Their vote may not represent their own interests but the interests of powerful adults.

Indeed, providing children the right to vote could actually disempower rather than empower them. Adults might no longer feel obliged to stand up for children's interests but would be free to compete with children politically in the same way they currently compete with each other. Furthermore, cultural and political leaders would have every incentive to use their greater economic and cultural power to manipulate children's voting behaviors in whatever ways they can. Mary John has shown that it was precisely to avoid adult manipulation that children were provided separate children's parliaments, using much the same logic as for separate juvenile justice systems.[31]

There are three reasons why this independence argument is still, however, not sufficient for denying children the right to vote.

First, it is inaccurate to divide the world into dependent children and independent adults. Adults too are deeply dependent on others: on relationships and families for support, on cultures for moral guidance, on shared economic systems, on mass media for information and interpretation, and much else. Humans can be manipulated in many ways. Studies have shown that husbands and wives tend to vote more similarly over time.[32] Eighteen- to twenty-one-year-olds in the United Kingdom vote for the same party as their parents 89 to 92 percent of the time.[33] Poor adults in the United States routinely vote against their own economic interests because of the political influence of corporate money and mass media.[34] As Franklin observes regarding children, "To isolate one group within society and insist that they alone should display the mythical qualities of latter-day Robinson Crusoes, or else be denied political rights, is unjust."[35]

Second, even if children are more dependent than adults in the private sphere, this does not necessarily mean they are more dependent in the public sphere. Many adults too are highly dependent in their private lives—such as those with severe physical disabilities or chronic illnesses, those who have lost or never had jobs, and the elderly—and no one suggests that therefore they should be denied the right to vote. In an argument for "the right to vote for people of any age," John Holt claims that "a society which had changed enough in its way of looking at young children to be willing to grant them the right to vote would be one in which few people would want or try to coerce a child's vote and in which most people would feel this was a very bad and wrong thing to do."[36] Dependency in the home does not necessarily equate to lack of independence in politics.

Finally, the dependence argument against children voting is somewhat circular. It denies children the political independence to vote because children are not politically independent. This strategy is familiar from the past. Women, minorities, and the poor were all denied the vote in part because of their supposed dependency on their husbands, ethnic "superiors," and landlords. As we already saw Iris Marion Young argue about women, "No persons, actions, or aspects of a person's life should be forced into privacy."[37] Likewise, children should not be forced out of the public sphere simply because they have certain dependencies in the private sphere. In a world dominated by adults, it is unfair to deny children the power to vote because of their existing lack of power. On the contrary, it is all the more reason to enfranchise them.

WOULD CHILDREN'S VOTING CAUSE HARM TO CHILDREN?

These three issues—of children's competence, knowledge, and independence to vote—are all about children's basic capacities. But there is another set of issues having to do with potential consequences. Would children voting cause harm to either children themselves or to the adults and societies around them? Let us consider each case in turn.

For children themselves, the harms that might result from their right to vote are several.

First, they could vote against their own interests. Their lack of experience in the world could mean that they either do not know what is best for themselves or cannot see what would be best for their own futures. As Locke argued long ago, "The necessities of [a child's] life, the health of his body, and the information of his mind would require him to be directed by the will of others and not his own."[38] Or, as Geoffrey Scarre has more recently put it, minors should not vote because "most adults, because they have lived a long time, have this ability [to plan systematic policies of action], but children, because their mental powers and experience are inadequate, do not."[39] Children might vote for representatives who promise, for example, to shorten the school day, lower the driving age, legalize underage sex, or remove parental controls from mass media.

Another kind of harm that could be caused to children is that the heavy responsibility of voting could rob them of their right to a free and playful childhood. This is why children are not generally given other kinds of adult responsibilities such as supporting themselves economically or making serious medical decisions. Ludvig Beckman argues that children should not be enfranchised because "voting is associated with shouldering a host of responsibilities" that undermine the more basic interest of children to engage in playful activities.[40]

Finally, it can be argued that even if children's right to vote is itself beneficial for children, it could start a slippery slope of new children's rights that are not. Once they could vote, children might demand further rights, such as to choose whether or not to attend school, to work full time, or to divorce their parents. Or the consequences could be more indirect. For example, as is already happening in the United States, minors might increasingly be tried for crimes as adults. As Martin Guggenheim summarizes this objection, the more children gain political rights, the less societies will "treat children like children."[41]

There are several possible counterarguments.

First, there is again a double standard. If adults potentially harm themselves by voting, this does not cancel their right to vote. And, indeed, clearly adults vote against their own best interests on a regular basis. As Franklin puts it, "That adults have an understanding of the interests of children which is superior to that possessed by the children themselves is not sufficient to justify intervention in their [political] affairs."[42] Contra Locke, today we normally consider the right to vote as belonging to citizens regardless of how badly they might use it. We value democratic inclusion over the potential resulting harms, trusting that the democratic process ultimately pays off.

Second, children's right to vote would not necessarily translate into adultlike rights in other areas. Adults would remain a majority of the voting population and still control more levers of political, economic, and cultural power. The right not to attend school, for example, would have to be supported by more than just children who do not like school. In general, voting does not prevent different groups from having different rights: such as the poor's rights to welfare, disabled persons' rights to accessibility, and the elderly's rights to health care. Simply because they could vote would not in itself deny children their special rights to a free education, economic support, a family, juvenile courts, and so on. On the contrary, children's special interests would likely gain even more political visibility.

Third and most important, far from doing them harm, suffrage would on the whole bring children and youth significant benefits. It would help to enlighten politicians about minors' actual lives and experiences, making it possible to make better-informed policies. And it would force politicians to provide children more full and equal consideration. Politicians are already supposed to represent children's interests; now they would be held to that duty more directly. They would feel much greater pressure, for example, to invest in schools, strengthen children's health insurance, provide support to parents, improve recreation spaces, reduce child poverty, combat labor exploitation, fight children's discrimination, and in general work for children's inclusion and dignity.

WOULD CHILDREN'S VOTING CAUSE HARM TO ADULTS AND SOCIETIES?

Even if children might benefit, would their voting harm adults? Would it undermine parents, set back the rights of women and the elderly, or even damage social and cultural systems? Would it unfairly give children power over adult interests?

When it comes to parents, the argument here is that they could find it more difficult to exercise their rightful authority over their offspring. For example, parents might find themselves less able to demand success in school, pass on their faith, set bedtimes, make medical decisions, and so on. Guggenheim argues that "attempting to consider the rights and needs of (very young) children without simultaneously taking into account the rights and needs of their parents is akin to attempting to isolate someone's arm from the rest of their body."[43] Children's well-being depends in large measure on their parents having the latitude to make decisions on children's behalf, sometimes against children's own immediate wishes. Children's suffrage could, in effect, replace parental authority with that of the state, as children increasingly gain the ability to use the ballot to circumvent parental control.

Beyond parents, children would gain a certain level of power over adults across society. Philip Cowley and David Denver point out that the child vote could undermine political wisdom, because children "have little experience of life beyond family and school, and no memory of governments or public affairs going back further than two or three years at most."[44] For example, children might roll back gains made by women by demanding parental time out of work to raise them. Or they might gain greater shares of government funding and health care that currently go toward the relatively smaller population of the elderly. In general, democracy requires everyone to submit to the shared power of the general population, and it is unfair for adults with greater experience and knowledge to submit to children with relatively little.

Finally, children voting could be viewed in the Global South as imposing a Eurocentric individualism. In more collectively oriented societies, child suffrage could undermine not only parental but also cultural hierarchies rooted in deep historical traditions. Some argue, for example, that the UN's growing interest in children's participation rights "may be more problematic in cultures where freedom of expression and self-assertion are less valued than obedience and duty fulfillment and where adult-child interactions are traditionally quite hierarchical."[45] Children's rights to vote could undermine communities.

While it is the one most cited, the argument concerning parental power is probably the least compelling one here. Private and public life only intersect to a point. If children were somehow able to ban parents from passing on their faith, for example, this would require both the will of significant numbers of adults (and children) and the overturning of fundamental constitutional and legal protections. What is more, parents will always hold more political power than children, since parents as a group will always hold more economic, cultural, historical, and social power to influence political life. Young people's suffrage would not overturn adult power so much as provide the least naturally powerful age group at least a measure of political balance.

It is already established that the state has a role in checking parental power, for example, when parents are abusive or neglectful. Minors' voting would make it easier to challenge adults' misuse of their power over children as well as uncover ways this misuse has so far remained hidden. Just as women voting arguably improved rather than worsened gender relations, so also would children voting improve age relations. For example, parents could find themselves required to be involved in schools, obliged to save for college, less protected in cases of sexual exploitation, or held to firmer responsibilities after divorce.

In addition, children voting would generally improve the lives of adults. Democracies are successful political systems because they enable the widest diversity of voices and experiences to influence political debate. The problem with authoritarianism of any kind is not that those in power are necessarily wrong. It is that they are not held accountable to alternative perspectives. And so they are less likely to reach justice and produce flourishing societies.

Children's suffrage would help policymakers, NGO leaders, teachers, doctors, and religious leaders—indeed, any public figure—to better understand and confront the diversity of children's issues and experiences. It should in principle enable them to perform their responsibilities more effectively. Adults would have more incentive and information, for example, to fight discrimination in schools, respond to disabilities, and develop effective health policies. As just one small example, the children's parliament in Barra Mansa, Brazil, successfully pressed for brighter lighting on unsafe streets, which made the streets safer for everyone, not just children.[46] Societies are interdependent networks. The wager of democracy is that a greater diversity of voices will on the whole produce more fully just and flourishing societies for all.

Finally, the cultural argument against children voting is somewhat paradoxical. It defends marginalizing one group—children—on the basis of the marginalization of another—adults of the Global South. The premise of anticolonialism is exactly the same premise on which children demand the vote: that those with less power should be heard. The postcolonial theorist Gayatri Chakravorty Spivak asks, "Can the subaltern speak?"—a question that should apply above all to Global South children.[47] What is more, children have in reality come closer to sharing in the vote in the Global South than they have in the Global North. Witness the powerful children's parliaments and child labor unions in countries such as India, Bolivia, Brazil, and Nigeria. Imagine if a Bangladeshi nine-year-old making clothing for the global corporation Forever 21 were to gain the power to vote.

CONCLUSION: A PROXY-CLAIM VOTE

Most people and scholars do not favor children's rights to vote. A few do. My own perspective is a childist one. I believe that the whole question should be reconsidered from a child-centered point of view. Children should have the right to vote, but the very nature of voting needs to be rethought as a consequence. We saw that as suffrage was extended over history from nobility to landowners, to all white men, to all men, and finally to all adults, the very meaning of voting also changed. It is today no longer a prerogative of aristocracy or a duty of heads of households. The same kind of shift in thinking will need to take place if suffrage is to be extended to the remaining third of humanity still excluded from it.

Theoretically speaking, democracy needs to recognize that persons are not just individually autonomous but differently interdependent. As I suggested toward the end of chapter 2, a more universal basis for human rights is not just human independence but rather human interdependence—its belonging to multiple networks of social interconnectivity. Childhood starkly exposes the reality that political life is a complex web of both mutual dependence and diverse independence. Even the most powerful CEO depends on an educated workforce, a functioning healthcare system, and the investments and supports of family, friends, and collaborators. Even the poorest newborn has his or her own desires, voice, and agency. Humans thrive and survive in the political realm when they are simultaneously supported by others and able to participate on their own terms.

Practically speaking, the best way to align democratic life with these shared human realities is by means of what I would call a "proxy-claim" right to vote.

This right would grant all citizens a "proxy" vote at birth to be used by a parent or guardian, then a "claim" vote at whatever time each citizen makes the choice to exercise the vote on his or her own behalf. Rather than either denying children the vote or simply extending the adult vote to them, a proxy-claim vote changes what it means to vote in order to provide equal representation for all, regardless of age.

This proposal is similar to the German parliament's proposal of 2008, with the important difference that rather than parents or guardians deciding when to give the vote to their child, the child herself decides when to claim it. As suggested by our discussion of voting competence earlier, persons can be considered ready to vote whenever they wish to claim the vote for themselves. Voting should remain, even for children, something available as a right rather than bestowed at the will of another.

Why an initial proxy vote?

There is a general argument against all proxy voting that says that it grants unjust power to the proxy and can be used for the proxy's own interests. But this argument does not recognize humans' political interdependency. Without a proxy vote, the youngest of children would end up (like all children in the current voting situation) with no political representation at all. Indeed, were older children able to claim the vote, younger children without a proxy vote would find themselves even more profoundly marginalized than they already are. A proxy vote ensures that even if a child has no idea what voting is—as in the case of infants and younger children—he or she still has a direct impact on political life through the extra vote gained by the person most able to use it in the child's best interest. He or she becomes politically empowered.

This proxy could also be extended to adults who may not be competent to vote, such as those with dementia, the severely mentally ill, and the chronically hospitalized. Perhaps it could also be extended to felons (though I'd argue it is more just not to take away their vote in the first place). When voting is thought about differently, it can be extended in different ways to adults as well. Indeed, it is worth remembering that all democratic voting is proxy in a way, since we vote for representatives who decide how to vote for laws and policies on our behalf.

Why a subsequent claim vote?

The current system in modern democracies is that citizens become entitled to vote at a certain age. In some countries such as the United States, citizens must register to vote to prove their eligibility. In others, eligibility is automatic. A claim vote would fall somewhere in between. Children would be able to claim their vote by a simple process, which may differ by country, of making known in public their desire to vote. It could not rely on extensive proofs of eligibility such as driver's licenses or identification cards, as children may not have them. It should face no higher barrier than, for example, registering for school or creating an account online.

It would also make sense for the claim vote to become automatic at a certain age or other marker. An age of automatic claim will vary from country to country, because children's relation to public life is also variable. But it should never be higher than fourteen. If fourteen-year-olds virtually everywhere can work and pay taxes, and if they are already active in political life around the world, they should be considered beyond the age where there is any question of their competence to vote.

There are numerous other questions that might be raised.

Which parent would have the proxy vote if a child has more than one parent or if the parents are separated? Possible solutions include letting the parents themselves decide; giving first choice to the parent having the greater child care responsibilities; dividing the proxy vote into two half-votes; or making the proxy vote the average of the vote of both parents.

Should schools be involved in the voting process? On the one hand, schools could be useful in making sure that all children learn about and exercise their voting rights. On the other hand, schools would insert a mediating institution into children's voting of a kind that is not present for adults, thus creating possibilities for teacher manipulation. And some children might attend more actively helpful schools than others, creating uneven advantages. Perhaps the best solution is for schools to be involved in voter education—since this fits with their educational mission—but not in actual voting itself, which is best conducted at the age-free sites used by adults.

Finally, and perhaps trickiest of all, if children gained the right to vote, should they therefore also have rights to hold elected office? On the one hand, minimum age requirements for elected office are supported by the idea that, unlike voting itself, holding office gives one extensive power over many people. The competencies and knowledge required should therefore be greater. The United States, for example, has age limits of twenty-five for the House of Representatives, thirty for the Senate, and thirty-five for the presidency. On the other hand, it might be possible for children to serve as representatives if doing so did not interfere with other rights such as to a full-time education. This would require changing the nature of elected office itself, including deprofessionalizing it or even, as in the early United States, making it purely voluntary. It might involve taking policymaking more fully online.

However these and other questions might be answered, any kind of proxy-claim vote would improve the political situation of children compared to where it is now. Children and youth are the only major social group still excluded from direct political representation. And this despite the fact that they are equally, if not more, affected by political decisions. Disenfranchising an entire class of citizens is unjust without significantly more compelling reasons for doing so. As I have hoped to show, children having rights to vote would better respect children's experiences and dignity, improve both their and adults' lives, and create significantly more democratic democracies.

7

TODAY'S GLOBAL CHALLENGE

Thirteen-year-old Tony Anderson is one of around four hundred thousand children living in foster care in the United States. He and his younger sister were removed from the home of his mentally ill mother due to medical neglect when he was four. The state attorney has now filed to terminate their mother's parental rights so that he and his sister can be put up for adoption. But Anderson himself, as well as his sister and their longtime foster parents, opposes terminating his mother's rights, as he wants to maintain contact and care for her when he is older and has a job. Unfortunately, unlike adults, minors in the United States have no due process rights to "standing" in court and so cannot themselves demand that their wishes be heard. "She's my mother, ain't she?" he declares in frustration. "Ain't I got rights?"[1]

Anderson's case provides a snapshot of the overall challenge confronting children's rights today.

On the one hand, children have more rights than at any time in history. Anderson has rights to a lawyer and a hearing and thinks of himself as a rights holder. He also has myriad other rights, such as to an education and protections against abuse. The children's rights movement of the past century or so is one of humanity's greatest achievements.

On the other hand, compared to adults, children are still legal, social, and political second-class citizens. Unlike if he were an adult, Anderson has no legal standing in court or right to hire his own lawyer. He also lacks many other rights, such as to democratic inclusion, guaranteed health insurance, protection from poverty, and equal freedoms of speech and assembly. In many ways, the children's rights movement lags behind the larger human rights movement. Children's rights are not yet fully human rights.

We have seen why children's rights are caught up in this kind of ambiguity.

In theoretical terms, rights have long been thought of as the kinds of things that belong primarily to adults. You have more rights, according to the usual thinking, if you are more independent, autonomous, and "rational." As a result, even if children are granted rights, they are granted them in secondhand ways and often regardless of children's own concrete experiences as children.

In practical terms, children's policy and law are historically recent developments that tend to take a backseat to the supposedly more serious public concerns of adults. Like for minority groups in the past, children's rights are up against long-entrenched adult power. The situation is doubly difficult for children because they often possess fewer economic and cultural resources to fight against their disempowerment in the first place.

All of this is to say that children's rights are today's global challenge.

Children's rights are not only a challenge *for* the world to enact but also a challenge *to* the world to reform itself. They present the twenty-first-century human rights community with its deepest possible self-critique. They challenge human rights to respond to the most disempowered third of humanity and so become truly human.

Put differently, the challenge is one of what I have been calling childism. Childism refers to the effort to restructure historically ingrained habits of thinking in response to children's long-submerged experiences. It means imagining human rights more broadly and inclusively—and therefore also differently. Rights have shifted in meaning over time in response to class, race, ethnicity, and gender, and it is now time for them to shift and expand again in response to the diverse realities of age.

This concluding chapter summarizes this challenge in two ways. First, it looks back at the children's rights questions and ambiguities that we have explored throughout this book. Then it maps out what it might take to create a better children's rights future. The past and the future are connected, since a more just world can only emerge out of the world as it comes to be formed. Children's rights need to be seen as part of human rights and their long struggle to expand social justice and the social imagination.

WHERE DO CHILDREN'S RIGHTS STAND TODAY?

Previous chapters have each in one way or another found that children's rights are a challenge because they remain ambiguous.

Chapter 1 examined the ways in which children's rights still leave them the world's most disadvantaged group.

Despite much progress in the past two hundred years, human rights remain profoundly divided according to age. In poor and wealthy countries alike, children are systematically poorer, less healthy, and more politically and legally marginalized than any other major group. The two main reasons for this situation are privatization and globalization. Children and youth live increasingly privatized lives within home and school while at the same time being increasingly more easily exploited for public gain in globalizing marketplaces and politics.

Children's rights, as a result, face the important challenge of including children as full members of the public world. Rights are the de facto global language, though not the only global language, for supporting and empowering persons in societies. Without rights, children are not treated with the full dignity and respect they deserve.

Chapter 2 explored the underlying reasons for children's secondary status in human rights theory.

We found that ideas about children's rights face a long and powerful tradition of understanding rights as only or primarily for adults. A right has always meant, in one way or another, a means of public empowerment. For millennia, only the monarchy truly held the right to power under the theory of the divine right of kings. Around a thousand years ago, the idea of rights started to spread to include first nobility and then landowners. And it eventually extended to include the poor, ethnic and racial minorities, and women. But it is only very recently that rights theorists have begun to imagine what it means for rights to belong also to children. In fact, the major rights philosophers of the Enlightenment explicitly argued that rights create a public realm only for adults. And even today, most major rights thinkers simply assume that it is adults they are primarily talking about.

Rights theory is beginning, however, to change. It is catching up, as it were, with longer-standing children's rights practices. Some contemporary theorists view children's rights as extensions of the rights of other marginalized groups, such as women and minorities. Others are developing ways to rethink human rights specifically in response to children. For example, rights might express people's interdependency rather than individuality or their diversity rather than sameness. In any case, new understandings are evolving of what it means for children to be empowered as full members of their societies, equally dignified persons deserving full support and participation in child-inclusive public worlds.

Chapter 3 looked at the ambiguities built into children's rights from the different angle of their historical development.

This development was described as having taken place in three waves that built upon each other. First, nineteenth- and early-twentieth-century children's rights primarily sought to guarantee children "the right to a childhood" by providing such things as relief from work and poverty and a free education. Post–World War II children's rights placed a new emphasis on children's rights to public protections, protections such as those against violence, abuse, and discrimination. And in the last two to three decades, following the new field of childhood studies and the 1989 Convention on the Rights of the Child, children's rights began to focus in addition on enabling children's active societal participation, such as through free speech, labor unions, judicial processes, citizenship, and political representation. These layers of provision, protection, and participation rights represent overall a movement from saving children as passive rights objects to also empowering children as active rights subjects.

The situation at our own particular historical moment is, as a result, incomplete but pregnant with possibility. Some areas of children's rights have made significant global progress, even if there is much work to be done: education, health care, non-abuse, nondiscrimination, aid and rescue, and other areas of provision and protection rights. Other areas of children's rights are newer and meet with greater obstacles: political participation, labor unions and parliaments, freedom of speech and assembly, judicial due process, and other forms of participation rights. But the tide is turning. For the more that children gain rights to influence public life, the more likely it is that their rights will grow overall.

The next three chapters took up specific examples of key children's rights issues today. There are countless other such issues that could be examined in detail. These include judicial rights, disability rights, sexual orientation rights, rights to life and survival, parents and a family, health care, leisure and play, nondiscrimination, non-abuse, a national and cultural identity, migrant and refugee status, freedom of speech, and freedom of religion, to name just a few. The three examples in this book are simply illustrative of the kinds of questions that might be asked within each of the broad categories of provision, protection, and participation rights.

Chapter 4 took up the example of children's rights to education.

Education is in a way the most distinctive right for children. It is an example of what is generally considered a provision right, a right to receive public support. But, as we saw, it is at the same time also a protection and a participation right. And, in a more general sense, it is an empowerment right: a right not only to future capabilities but also to realizing capabilities in each child's here and now. Key questions here include whether education is a right at all; whether the right should be universal; whether it demands equality; what in fact it is a right to; and in what senses children should have rights to make their own educational choices.

Education rights turn out not just to be entitlements provided by adults but, more profoundly, means for empowering children as children. This is the view suggested by Malala Yousafzai in her campaign for educational rights for girls. The most successful education rights, such as in Finland and New Zealand, focus less on reaching eventual adult goals than on the encouragement of children's own energies and creativity. Education rights must strike a difficult balance between sufficient societal investment of resources and respect for children's dignity and differences as children.

Chapter 5 considered the equally complex rights of child slaves.

Slave labor is an obvious violation of protection rights, rights against being harmed or exploited by others. There are an estimated 5.5 million children worldwide today working in slave conditions in areas such as domestic servitude, industrial labor, agriculture, street vending, sex work, and soldiering. Despite being illegal worldwide, the reality on the ground is that it is now easier under globalization to exploit children's slave labor than ever before. Important questions include how child slavery is defined; how it has changed under globalization; when child labor becomes truly exploitative; and what remedies are effective in terms of both specific legal and broader human rights.

It turns out that children in such situations need to be viewed as more than just victims requiring protection. They are also agents deserving rights to support and empowerment. They stand in this sense in the same situation as adult slaves: needing rights to fully dignified inclusion in the whole of society. What becomes especially clear when one considers children is that freedom from slavery is not just a matter of being restored to independence. It is more profoundly a matter, for children and adults both, of being fully and fairly included in the globe's systems of economic interdependence.

Finally, chapter 6 considered the particularly controversial question of whether children should have the right to vote.

Suffrage has only very recently been considered a potential right for children, and many scholars and activists oppose it. It is an example of participation rights, rights to speak and act in public on one's own behalf. Voting is a right to influence one's society's very system of rights, and, as such, is perhaps the ultimate test of what it might mean for children to be publicly empowered.

Here we looked into questions of why children have historically been denied the vote; whether children are sufficiently competent, knowledgeable, and independent to do so; whether children's voting would cause harm to children themselves, adults, or society; and what implications child suffrage would have for the meaning and practice of suffrage overall.

Here I presented my own ideas for not only why children should gain the right to vote but also why the right to vote itself should accordingly be thought about and enacted differently for all. In contrast with those who oppose a child vote, as well as those who would simply extend to children the same right to vote as adults, I defended a childist argument that all suffrage, child and adult alike, should be based on a new kind of proxy-claim vote. All citizens deserve the right to a proxy vote at birth, as well as at any time they cannot exercise it for themselves, granted to a parent or guardian; and all citizens equally deserve the right to claim their vote to exercise on their own behalf at any time they choose. There are many possible objections to such a view. But, at the very least, I hope I showed why children's suffrage is an important issue to discuss.

TOWARD WHAT FUTURE?

If such is the situation of the children's rights movement today, where might it go in the future?

It is clear from both past history and today's situation that children's rights need to move beyond a narrow focus on children being saved and protected by adults toward a broad embrace of children's inclusion and empowerment as children.

What makes a right a right is that it confers a measure of public capacity or power. But, as children show, this power can take many different forms. It can mean the right to take part in social, economic, and political freedoms. Participation rights use public power directly. But it can also mean the right to be provided with public resources, such as an education, health care, and social security. Provision rights empower citizens indirectly by giving them the networks of support they need to succeed in the world. And power can also mean the right to protections against such things as harm, discrimination, abuse, and violence. Protection rights empower by resisting the ways that persons can be disempowered by others.

In other words, rights are means to empower persons in diverse ways as interdependent members of societies.

Different groups in different societies doubtless require different combinations of these kinds of rights. But all groups depend on some amalgamation of all three. Those of us who think of ourselves as adults belong to webs of public rights that give us freedoms, resources, and protections in different combinations, depending on whether we are young or elderly, wealthy or poor, healthy or sick, and so on. The same is the case for children, and again in different ways for different children. Rights overall have the goal of guaranteeing, by whatever means, all groups' maximum public empowerment.

The question for the future of children's rights is, then, what particular configuration of rights will help to empower or include children most fully.

When it comes to provision types of rights, children worldwide are still systematically denied a fair proportion of public and social resources. Despite much progress, young people are still every country's poorest group and still receive deeply inadequate investments in such vital needs as health care, economic security, and education. In part, children's provision rights depend on their protection rights against class, gender, and ultimately age discrimination, as well as participation rights to make their needs and voices properly heard. But mostly they depend on societies meeting their basic obligations to invest sufficient resources in their young.

In terms of protection rights, children and youth need to be recognized as equally if not more vulnerable to individual and systemic harm. Young people experience physical and sexual abuse, labor exploitation, sex trafficking, racial discrimination, judicial injustice, wartime violence, and much else that violates their dignity as human beings. Part of the solution again lies in increased children's rights in other areas, such as adequate provisions for health and education and opportunities to participate and have voices in society. But primarily the solution lies in acknowledging that children do not live in a separate, private sphere but are owed as least as strong a public network as adults of legal, cultural, and political protections. And if children are vulnerable to harm from others, this is not just a childlike condition but shines a light on the human condition as such.

It is in the area of children's participation rights that the most needs to be done. The reality is that for children just as for adults, participation rights are ultimately the key to gaining improved rights overall. It is true in part, again, that participation rights rely on other kinds of rights, such as protections against discrimination and provisions of education and resources. But without a renewed focus on children's participation rights, such as to voices, agency, and recognition in the public world, children will never escape their historical status as second-class citizens. Children's public participation may not end up looking exactly the same as adults'. And adults' modes of public participation may also have to change. But in one way or another, children both deserve and need to play an equal part in shaping public life.

Through these and other means, children's rights might transcend their somewhat dehumanizing history of serving primarily as means for children to be saved by adults. In this model, only those defined as adults are empowered subjects, and those defined as children are their dependent objects. Children will fully gain their rights only to the extent that their rights do what rights are meant to do—namely, include them as equal public citizens.

Exactly how children may be included in practice remains an open question, one to be answered in part by children themselves. Like adults' rights, children's rights will take different forms in different contexts and cultures. But the future of children's rights should be focused on creating diverse combinations of particular rights that gradually overturn children's deep historical disempowerment.

The greatest challenge of the children's rights movement is to expand and reshape human rights to finally achieve their promised humanity. Perhaps children's rights will also help in rethinking the rights of animals and the biosphere too, beings with whom humans also share a profound interdependence. The humanization of children's rights is the same thing as the "childization" of human rights. The world is changing in response to the diverse experiences of gender, sexuality, class, race, and ethnicity. What if it also changed in response to the diverse experiences of age? What if all children were as empowered to change their societies as the nine-year-old parliamentarian Tazim Ali? The world would be a very different place indeed.

NOTES

I. WHY CHILDREN'S RIGHTS

1. Emily Wax, "When the Little Ones Run the Show," *Washington Post*, May 14, 2009, accessed September 8, 2014, http://www. washingtonpost.com/wp-dyn/content/article/2009/05/13/ AR2009051303758.html. See also Kulsum Mustafa, "Children's Parliament Held in Central Hall, Uttar Pradesh Legislative Assembly Shows the Way," UNICEF 2008, accessed September 8, 2014, http://www. unicef.org/india/child_protection_4703.htm.

2. John Wall, *Ethics in Light of Childhood* (Washington, DC: Georgetown University Press, 2010), 3. The term "childism" can also be used in an opposed, negative sense to refer to children's oppression, in analogy to terms like "racism" and "sexism." However, I prefer the positive sense, in analogy to feminism, of trying to take children's lives into fuller account.

3. United Nations Population Division, *World Population Prospects: The 2015 Revision*, "Population by Broad Age Groups—Both Sexes," accessed June 1, 2016, http://esa.un.org/unpd/wpp.

4. Alma Gottlieb, *The Afterlife Is Where We Come From: The Culture of Infancy in West Africa* (Chicago: University of Chicago Press, 2015).

5. United Nations Children's Fund (UNICEF), "Children Living in Poverty: Overview of Definitions, Measurements, and Policy" (New York: UNICEF Global Policy Section, 2006), 11.

6. United Nations Children's Fund (UNICEF), "Measuring Child Poverty: New League Tables of Child Poverty in the World's Rich Countries" (Florence, Italy: UNICEF Innocenti Research Centre, 2012), 21.

7. Iris Marion Young, *Justice and the Politics of Difference* (Princeton, NJ: Princeton University Press, 1990), 120.

8. World Health Organization (WHO), "Classification of Female Genital Mutilation," accessed July 26, 2016, http://www.who.int/reproductivehealth/topics/fgm/overview/en.

9. Jacqueline Bhaba, *Child Migration and Human Rights in a Global Age* (Princeton, NJ: Princeton University Press, 2014).

2. THEORETICAL CONTROVERSIES

1. Myra Bluebond-Langner, *The Private Worlds of Dying Children* (Princeton, NJ: Princeton University Press, 1978), 113–17.

2. Ibid., 135, 198.

3. John Locke, *Two Treatises of Government*, rev. ed., ed. Peter Laslett (New York: Cambridge University Press, 1960), II.II.4–6 (309–11), II.V.25–36 (327–35), II.VI.52–80 (345–63).

4. John Locke, *Some Thoughts concerning Education*, in *The Clarendon Edition of the Works of John Locke*, ed. J. W. Yolton and J. S. Yolton (New York: Oxford University Press, 1989), chapter 1, 83 and chapter 36, 105; Locke, *Essay concerning Human Understanding* (New York: Oxford University Press, 1975), I.I.27, II.I.6–8 and 20–22, and II.IX.5.

5. Jean-Jacques Rousseau, *The Social Contract*, trans. Maurice Cranston (New York: Penguin Books, 1968), II.1, 69–70.

6. Jean-Jacques Rousseau, *Emile, or On Education*, trans. Allan Bloom (New York: Basic, 1979), 37; see also Rousseau, *The Social Contract*, I.2, 50–51 and I.4, 54–55.

7. Immanuel Kant, *Foundations of the Metaphysics of Morals*, 2nd ed., trans. Lewis White Beck (Englewood Cliffs, NJ: Prentice-Hall, 1990), 47; and Immanuel Kant, *The Science of Right*, trans. W. Hastie (Clifton, NJ: A. M. Kelley, 1974), Introduction B–C.

8. Immanuel Kant, *Education*, trans. Annette Churton (Ann Arbor: University of Michigan Press, 1960).

9. Kant, *The Science of Right*, para. 28.

10. Kristin Herzog, *Children and Our Global Future: Theological and Social Challenges* (Cleveland, OH: Pilgrim, 2005), 74–83.

11. International Labour Organization, International Programme on the Elimination of Child Labour (IPEC), *Marking Progress against Child Labour: Global Estimates and Trends 2000–2012* (Geneva: ILO, 2013). See also Eric V. Edmonds and Nina Pavcnik, "Child Labor in the Global Economy," *Journal of Economic Perspectives* 19, no. 1 (2005): 199–220.

12. H. L. A. Hart, "Are There Any Natural Rights?," *Philosophical Review* 64 (1955): 175–91, 175.

13. John Rawls, *A Theory of Justice*, rev. ed. (Cambridge, MA: Harvard University Press, 1999), 53.

14. John Finnis, *Natural Law and Natural Rights* (New York: Oxford University Press, 1980).

15. Martha Nussbaum, *Sex and Social Justice* (New York: Oxford University Press, 1999), 40–41.

16. Sarada Balagopalan, "The Politics of Failure: Street Children and the Circulation of Rights Discourses in Kolkata (Calcutta), India," in *Reconceptualizing Children's Rights in International Development: Living Rights, Social Justice, Translations*, ed. Karl Hanson and Olga Nieuwenhuys (New York: Cambridge University Press, 2013), 133–51.

17. Gayatri Chakravorty Spivak, *A Critique of Postcolonial Reason: Toward a History of the Vanishing Present* (Cambridge, MA: Harvard University Press, 1999).

18. Martha Nussbaum, *In Defense of Universal Values*, Occasional Paper Series 16:OP:1 (Notre Dame, IN: Joan B. Kroc Institute for International Peace Studies, University of Notre Dame, 1999), 63.

19. Seyla Benhabib, *The Rights of Others: Aliens, Residents, and Citizens* (New York: Cambridge University Press, 2004), 179.

20. Arjun Appadurai, *The Future as Cultural Fact: Essays on the Global Condition* (London: Verso, 2013), 295.

21. Barbara Bennett Woodhouse, *Hidden in Plain Sight: The Tragedy of Children's Rights from Ben Franklin to Lionel Tate* (Princeton, NJ: Princeton University Press, 2008), 35. Similar approaches can also be found in Tom Cockburn, "Children as Participative Citizens: A Radical Pluralist Case for 'Child-Friendly' Public Communication," *Journal of Social Sciences* Special Issue no. 9 (2005): 19–29; and Marc Jans,

"Children as Citizens: Towards a Contemporary Notion of Child Participation," *Childhood* 11, no. 1 (2004): 27–44.

22. Ruth Lister, "Citizenship: Towards a Feminist Synthesis," *Feminist Review* 57 (1997): 28–48, 39.

23. Ruth Lister, "Why Citizenship: Where, When and How Children?" *Theoretical Inquiries in Law* 8, no. 2 (2007): 693–718.

24. John Wall, *Ethics in Light of Childhood* (Washington, DC: Georgetown University Press, 2010), 138.

3. HISTORICAL AMBIGUITIES

1. Patrick Thorman, "Child and Forced Labor in Tobacco's Killing Fields of Kazakhstan," *Regent Journal of International Law* 9 (2013): 213–45; see also Human Rights Watch, *"Hellish Work": Exploitation of Migrant Tobacco Workers in Kazakhstan* (New York: Human Rights Watch, 2010), accessed September 26, 2014, http://www.hrw.org/sites/default/files/reports/kazakhstan0710webwcover_1.pdf.

2. Kate Douglas Wiggin, *Children's Rights: A Book of Nursery Logic* (Amazon Digital Services, 2012; originally published New York, 1892), location 68.

3. E. Royston Pike, *Human Documents of the Industrial Revolution in Britain* (Boston: George Allen & Unwin, 1966), 101–77.

4. Ashba Bajpai, *Child Rights in India: Law, Policy, and Practice* (New York: Oxford University Press, 2003), 159.

5. Brian Platt, "Japanese Childhood, Modern Childhood: The Nation-State, the School, and 19th-Century Globalization," *Journal of Social History* 38, no. 4 (Summer 2005): 965–85, 973, 978.

6. Bajpai, *Child Rights in India*, 334.

7. A. Platt, *The Child Savers: The Invention of Delinquency* (Chicago: University of Chicago Press, 1969).

8. Hugh Cunningham, *The Invention of Childhood* (London: BBC Books, 2006), 15.

9. United Nations, Charter of the United Nations, "Preamble," June 26, 1945, accessed November 3, 2015, http://www.un.org/en/charter-united-nations.

10. See UN General Assembly, Resolution 55/2, "United Nations Millennium Declaration," September 8, 2000, accessed November 3, 2015, http://www.un.org/millennium/declaration/ares552e.htm.

11. Allison James and Alan Prout, "Introduction," in *Constructing and Reconstructing Childhood*, 2nd ed., ed. Allison James and Alan Prout (New York: Routledge, 1997), 4.

12. Mary John, *Children's Rights and Power: Charging Up for a New Century* (London: Jessica Kingsley, 2003), 45–46.

13. Ann Quennerstedt, "Children, But Not Really Humans? Critical Reflections on the Hampering Effect of the '3 p's,'" *International Journal of Children's Rights* 18 (2010): 619–35, 629.

4. EDUCATION IN AN AGE
OF GLOBALIZATION

1. UNESCO Institute for Statistics, "Progress in Getting All Children to School Stalls but Some Countries Show the Way Forward" (Policy Paper 14, Fact Sheet 28, June 2014); and UNESCO Center for Statistics, "Adjusted Net Enrolment Rate by Level of Education," accessed January 15, 2015, http://data.uis.unesco.org/index.aspx?queryid=145&lang=en.

2. UNESCO Center for Statistics, "Progress," "Adjusted Net Enrolment."

3. Carlos Nava is an invented composite taken, along with the above statistics, from Jean Grugel and Frederico Poley Martins Ferreira, "Street Working Children's Agency and the Challenge of Children's Rights: Evidence from Minas Gerais, Brazil," *Journal of International Development* 24 (2012): 828–40.

4. Katarina Tomasevski, *Human Rights Obligations in Education* (Enfield, NH: Enfield, 2006). See also Tomasevski, "The State of the Right to Education Worldwide: Free or Fee; 2006 Global Report" (Child Right Information Network [CRIN], Copenhagen, 2006), accessed July 27, 2016, https://www.crin.org/en/docs/katarina_tom_global.pdf.

5. Jody Heymann, Amy Raub, and Adèle Cassola, "Constitutional Rights to Education and Their Relationship to National Policy and

School Enrollment," *International Journal of Educational Development* 39 (2014): 131–41.

6. Heymann, Raub, and Cassola, "Constitutional Rights to Education."

7. Asha Bajpai, *Child Rights in India: Law, Policy, and Practice* (New York: Oxford University Press, 2003), 335.

8. Mona Kaushal, "Implementation of Right to Education in India: Issues and Concerns," *Journal of Management & Public Policy* 4, no. 1 (December 2012): 42–48.

9. Katarina Tomasevski, "Globalizing What: Education as a Human Right or as a Traded Service," *Indiana Journal of Global Legal Studies* 12, no. 1 (2005): 1–78, 3.

10. John-Stewart Gordon, "Is *Inclusive* Education a Human Right?" *Journal of Law, Medicine & Ethics* 41, no. 4 (Winter 2013): 754–67, 764.

11. Aman Ullah, "Right to Free and Compulsory Education in Pakistan after the 18th Constitutional Amendment," *South Asian Studies* 28, no. 2 (2013): 329–40, 340.

12. Tomasevski, "Globalizing What," 73–74.

13. "Complete 2014 Rankings of 339 Public High Schools," *New Jersey Monthly*, September 2, 2014.

14. Associated Press via NJ.com, "Only 3 Students Scored College-Ready in Camden," December 18, 2013.

15. Education Law Center, "Tracking Progress, Engaging Communities: Abbott Indicators Summary Report; Camden, NJ" (Newark, NJ: Education Law Center, 2005), 23.

16. Stephen Danley, "Did You Wear Thermals to Work Today? This Camden High Teacher Did," *Local Knowledge Blog*, January 8, 2015, accessed January 27, 2015, http://danley.camden.rutgers.edu/2015/01/08/did-you-wear-thermals-to-work-today-this-camden-high-teacher-did.

17. Harry Wilson, "Turning Off the School-to-Prison Pipeline," *Reclaiming Children & Youth* 23, no. 1 (Spring 2014): 49–53.

18. Michelle Alexander, *The New Jim Crow: Mass Incarceration in the Age of Colorblindness* (New York: The New Press, 2012), 6–7.

19. "Camden, New Jersey," *Wikipedia*, accessed January 15, 2015, http://en.wikipedia.org/wiki/Camden,_New_Jersey.

20. Tomasevski, "Globalizing What," 2–3.

21. UNESCO, *Teaching and Learning: Achieving Quality for All; EFA Global Monitoring Report 2013/4* (Paris: UNESCO, 2014), 2, 3.

22. United Nations Development Programme, *Human Development Report 2010: The Real Wealth of Nations; Pathways to Human Development* (New York: Palgrave Macmillan, 2010), 40, http://issuu.com/undphr/docs/human_development_report_2010.

23. UNESCO, *Teaching and Learning*, i, 3.

24. Rhys Griffith, *Educational Citizenship and Independent Learning* (London: Jessica Kingsley, 1998), 9.

25. Bruno Baronnet and Mariana Ortega Breña, "Rebel Youth and Zapatista Autonomous Education," *Latin American Perspectives* 35, no. 4 (July 2008): 112–24, 117.

26. Cindi Katz, *Growing Up Global: Economic Restructuring and Children's Everyday Lives* (Minneapolis: University of Minnesota Press, 2004), 113–17.

27. Elaine Unterhalter, Jo Heslop, and Andrew Mamedu, "Girls Claiming Education Rights: Reflections on Distribution, Empowerment and Gender Justice in Northern Tanzania and Northern Nigeria," *International Journal of Educational Development* 33 (2013): 566–75, 567.

28. Joan DeJaeghere, Jenny Parkes, and Elaine Unterhalter, "Editorial," *International Journal of Educational Development* 33 (2013): 539–45, 543.

29. UNESCO, *Teaching and Learning*, i.

30. Diane Ravitch, *The Death and Life of the Great American School System: How Testing and Choice Are Undermining Education*, rev. and exp. ed. (New York: Basic, 2011).

31. Ann Quennerstedt, "The Political Construction of Children's Rights in Education—A Comparative Analysis of Sweden and New Zealand," *Education Inquiry* 2, no. 3 (September 2011): 453–71, 461.

32. Anne B. Smith, "Children and Young People's Participation Rights in Education," *International Journal of Children's Rights* 15 (2007): 147–64, 155. See also L. Blaiklock, "Te Whāriki, the New Zealand Early Childhood Curriculum: Is It Effective?" *International Journal of Early Years Education* 18 (2010): 201–12.

33. Irene Rizzini and Nisha Thapliyal, "The Role of Schools in the Protection and Promotion of Children's Rights in Brazil" (unpublished

paper, CIESPI, Rio de Janeiro, 2005), 18, cited in Smith, "Children and Young People's Participation Rights," 149.

34. Quennerstedt, "Political Construction of Children's Rights," 675.

35. Pauline Tapp, "Children's Views on Children's Rights: 'You Don't Have Rights, You Only Have Privileges,'" *Childrenz Issues* 1, no. 1 (1997): 7–8; Dominic Wyse, "Felt Tip Pens and School Councils: Children's Participation Rights in Four English Schools," *Children & Society* 15 (2001): 209–18; Michael Wyness, "Regulating Participation: The Possibilities and Limits of Children and Young People's Councils," special issue no. 9, *Journal of Social Sciences* (2005): 7–18.

36. N. J. Taylor, A. B. Smith, and K. Nairn, "Rights Important to Young People: Secondary Student and Staff Perspectives," *International Journal of Children's Rights* 9, no. 2 (2001): 137–56.

37. Harry Shier, "Pathways to Participation: Openings, Opportunities and Obligations," *Children and Society* 10 (2001): 107–17. See also the earlier model of Roger Hart, "Children's Participation: From Tokenism to Citizenship" (report, UNICEF International Child Development Centre, Florence, Italy, 1992).

5. THE NEW CHILD SLAVERY

1. International Labour Organization (ILO), International Programme on the Elimination of Child Labour (IPEC), *Marking Progress against Child Labour: Global Estimates and Trends 2000–2012* (Geneva: ILO, 2013), 21–22.

2. Kevin Bales, *Ending Slavery: How We Free Today's Slaves* (Berkeley: University of California Press, 2008), 9.

3. Free the Slaves, "Trafficking and Slavery Fact Sheet," accessed January 6, 2014, http://www.freetheslaves.net/document.doc?id=34.

4. Anti-Slavery Society, "Does Slavery Still Exist?," accessed January 6, 2014, http://www.anti-slaverysociety.org/slavery.htm.

5. Ark of Hope for Children, "Child Trafficking Statistics," accessed January 9, 2014, http://www.arkofhopeforchildren.org/issues/child-trafficking-statistics#.Us8Nbfssx_c); Cheryl Nelson Butler, "Sex Slavery in the Lone Star State: Does the Texas Human Trafficking Legislation of 2011 Protect Minors?" *Akron Law Review* 45 (2012): 843–82, 844.

6. Linda A. Smith, Samantha Healy Vardama, and Melissa A. Snow, "The National Report on Domestic Minor Sex Trafficking: America's Prostituted Children" (report, Shared Hope International, Vancouver, WA, 2009), 8.

7. Smith, Vardama, and Snow, "National Report on Domestic Minor Sex Trafficking," 14.

8. Smith, Vardama, and Snow, "National Report on Domestic Minor Sex Trafficking," 15.

9. United Nations, Office of the High Commissioner for Human Rights, Slavery Convention (accessed May 2015, http://www.ohchr.org/EN/ProfessionalInterest/Pages/SlaveryConvention.aspx).

10. International Labour Organization (ILO), "Forced Labour Convention No. 29 (1930)," accessed January 6, 2014, http://www.ilo.org/dyn/normlex/en/f?p=NORMLEXPUB:12100:0::NO::P12100_ILO_CODE:C029.

11. International Labour Organization (ILO), "Abolition of Forced Labor Convention, 1957 (No. 105)," accessed May 2015, http://www.ilo.org/dyn/normlex/en/f?p=NORMLEXPUB:12100:0::NO:12100:P12100_INSTRUMENT_ID:312250:NO.

12. United Nations, "International Covenant on Civil and Political Rights" (1966), accessed January 6, 2014, http://www.ohchr.org/en/professionalinterest/pages/ccpr.aspx.

13. Free the Slaves, "Trafficking and Slavery Fact Sheet," accessed May 2015, https://www.freetheslaves.net/wp-content/uploads/2015/01/FTS_factsheet-Nov17.21.pdf.

14. Mike Dotteridge, "Contemporary Child Slavery," in *Child Slaves in the Modern World*, ed. Gwyn Campbell, Suzanne Miers, and Joseph C. Miller (Athens: Ohio University Press, 2011), 254–67, 258.

15. International Labour Organization (ILO), "Helping Hands or Shackled Lives? Understanding Child Domestic Labour and Responses to It" (report, ILO, Geneva, 2004), iii, accessed January 9, 2014, http://www.ilo.org/wcmsp5/groups/public/---ed_norm/---ipec/documents/publication/kd00098.pdf.

16. Bridgett Carr, "Examining the Reality of Foreign National Child Victims of Human Trafficking in the United States," *Journal of Law and Policy* 37 (2011):183–204, 185; Philip Whalen and Malika Id'Salah, "Girls as Domestic Slaves in Contemporary France," in *Child Slaves in*

the Modern World, ed. Gwyn Campbell, Suzanne Miers, and Joseph C. Miller (Athens: Ohio University Press, 2011), 208–20, 212.

17. Jonathan Blagbrough, "This Is Nothing but Slavery: Child Domestic Labor in the Modern Context," in *Child Slaves in the Modern World*, ed. Joseph C. Miller, Suzanne Miers, and Gwyn Campbell (Athens: Ohio University Press, 2011), 193–207, 195.

18. Blagbrough, "This Is Nothing but Slavery," 200.

19. Cecilia Flores Oebanda, "Child Slavery in South and South East Asia," in *Child Slavery Now: A Contemporary Reader*, ed. Gary Craig (Portland, OR: Policy, 2010), 285–95, 292.

20. Kari B. Jensen, "Child Slavery and the Fish Processing Industry in Bangladesh," *Focus on Geography* 56, no. 2 (2013): 54–65, 55–61.

21. Dotteridge, "Contemporary Child Slavery," 261.

22. April Rieger, "Missing the Mark: Why the Trafficking Victims Protection Act Fails to Protect Sex Trafficking Victims in the United States," *Harvard Journal of Law and Gender* 30 (2007): 231–56, 231–32.

23. Emily K. Harlan, "It Happens in the Dark: Examining Current Obstacles to Identifying and Rehabilitating Child Sex Trafficking Victims in India and the United States," *University of Colorado Law Review* 83 (2012): 1113–47, 1124–25.

24. Kimberly Kotrla, "Domestic Minor Sex Trafficking in the United States," *Social Work* 55, no. 2 (April 2010), 181–87, 182.

25. Polaris Project, "Domestic Sex Trafficking: The Criminal Operations of the American Pimp; A Condensed Guide for Service Providers and Law Enforcement," accessed September 2013, http://www.polarisproject.org/resources/resources-by-topic/sex-trafficking, cited in V. Jordan Greenbaum, "Commercial Sexual Exploitation and Sex Trafficking of Children in the United States," *Current Problems in Pediatric Adolescent Health Care* 44 (October 2014): 245–269.

26. Sarah Maguire, "Children, Slavery, and Soldiering," in *Child Slaves in the Modern World*, ed. Gwyn Campbell, Suzanne Miers, and Joseph C. Miller (Athens: Ohio University Press, 2011), 238–53.

27. Hans van de Glind, "Child Trafficking: A Modern Form of Slavery," in *Child Slavery Now: A Contemporary Reader*, ed. Gary Craig (Portland, OR: Policy, 2010), 99–116.

28. Serdar M. Degirmencioglu, Hakan Acar, and Yüksel Baykara Acar, "Extreme Forms of Child Labour in Turkey," in *Child Slavery*

Now: A Contemporary Reader, ed. Gary Craig (Portland, OR: Policy, 2010), 215–26.

29. J. Lawrence French and Richard E. Wokutch, "Child Workers, Globalization, and International Business Ethics: A Case Study in Brazil's Export-Oriented Shoe Industry," *Business Ethics Quarterly* 15, no. 4 (2005): 615–64.

30. French and Wokutch, "Child Workers, Globalization, and International Business Ethics," 631.

31. Katie Wendle, "Establishing Liability for the Enslavement and Forced Labor of Children under the Alien Tort Statute," *Syracuse Journal of International Law and Commerce* 41, no. 2 (2014): 447–83, 476–79.

32. Sarah Murillo, "21st Century Slaves: Children Reduced to Products—Captured in the Business of Supply and Demand," *Phoenix Law Review* 6 (2013): 695–733, 696–97.

33. Hans van de Glind and Joost Kooijmans, "Modern-Day Child Slavery," *Children & Society* 22 (2008): 150–66, 156.

34. French and Wokutch, "Child Workers, Globalization, and International Business Ethics," 618–21.

35. Free the Slaves, "Slavery Today," accessed June 1, 2015, http://www.freetheslaves.net/about-slavery/slavery-today.

36. French and Wokutch, "Child Workers, Globalization, and International Business Ethics," 619.

37. Jagdish Bhagwati, *In Defense of Globalization* (New York: Oxford University Press, 2007), 69–71.

38. Nicola Phillips, "Unfree Labor and Adverse Incorporation in the Global Economy: Comparative Perspectives in Brazil and India," *Economy and Society* 42, no. 2 (2013): 171–96, 185.

39. World Social Forum, "Charter of Principles," principle 4 (2002), accessed January 14, 2014, http://www.forumsocialmundial.org.br/main.php?id_menu=4&cd_language=2).

40. M. Liebel, "Working Children as Social Subjects: The Contribution of Social Children's Organizations to Social Transformations," *Childhood* 10 (2003): 265–85.

41. French and Wokutch, "Child Workers, Globalization, and International Business Ethics," 635.

42. Matías Cordero Arce, "Towards an Emancipatory Discourse of Children's Rights," *International Journal of Children's Rights* 20 (2012): 365–421, 410.

43. Arce, "Towards an Emancipatory Discourse," 408–9.

44. Ishmael Beah, *A Long Way Gone: Memoirs of a Boy Soldier* (New York: Farrar, Straus and Giroux, 2007), 126, 169.

45. David Rosen, *Armies of the Young: Child Soldiers in War and Terrorism* (New Brunswick, NJ: Rutgers University Press, 2005).

46. Claire Breen, "When Is a Child Not a Child? Child Soldiers in International Law," *Human Rights Review* (January–March 2007): 71–103.

47. See, respectively: United States Code, Title 10, Section 2031; and United States Department of Defense, "Policy Memorandum 50—U.S. Army Recruiting Command (USAREC) Partnership Initiatives," 30 March 1999, accessed June 8, 2015, http://www.projectyano.org/pdf/JROTC_military_recruiting_memo.pdf.

48. US Army Junior Reserve Officer Training Corps, accessed June 2015, http://www.usarmyjrotc.com.

49. Karen Houppert, "Who's Next?" *Nation*, August 25, 2005.

50. United States Government Accountability Office (GAO), "Military Recruiting: DOD and Services Need Better Data to Enhance Visibility over Recruiter Irregularities" (report GAO-06-846, August 14, 2006), 2, 3, 30–33.

51. International Criminal Court, "Case Information Sheet: *The Prosecutor v. Thomas Lubanga Dyilo*," updated March 25, 2015, accessed June 4, 2015, http://www.icc-cpi.int/iccdocs/PIDS/publications/LubangaENG.pdf.

52. International Committee of the Red Cross, "The Paris Commitments to Protect Children from Unlawful Recruitment or Use by Armed Forces or Armed Groups," accessed June 4, 2015, https://www.icrc.org/eng/assets/files/other/pariscommitments_en.pdf.

53. International Criminal Court, "Case Information Sheet."

54. Joseph Rikhof, "Child Soldiers: Protection or Responsibility," in *Children and Armed Conflict*, ed. Daniel Thomas Cook and John Wall (New York: Palgrave Macmillan, 2011), 171–88, 178–83.

55. Center for the Study of Human Rights in the Americas, University of California, Davis, "Guantanamo's Children: The Wikileaked Testimonies," accessed June 10, 2015, http://humanrights.ucdavis.edu/

reports/guantanamos-children-the-wikileaked-testimonies/
guantanamos-children-the-wikileaked-testimonies.

56. Rikhof, "Child Soldiers: Protection or Responsibility," 183–87.

57. Lee Tucker, "Child Slaves in Modern India: The Bonded Labor
Problem," *Human Rights Quarterly* 19, no. 3 (August 1997): 572–629,
587–92.

58. Amrita Datta and Preet Rustagi, *Status of Women in Bihar: Exploring Transformation in Work and Gender Relations* (New Delhi:
Mimeo, Institute for Human Development, 2010), 31.

59. Shaziah Wasiuzzaman and Karen Wells, "Assembling Webs of
Support: Child Domestic Workers in India," *Children & Society* 24
(2010): 282–92, 290.

60. Treena Rae Orchard, "Girl, Woman, Lover, Mother: Towards a
New Understanding of Child Prostitution among Young Devadasis in
Rural Karnataka, India," *Social Science and Medicine* 64 (2007):
2379–90, 2388; see also Zosa de Sas Kropiwnicki, "Strategic Agents:
Adolescent Prostitutes in Cape Town, South Africa," in *Child Slaves in
the Modern World*, ed. Gwyn Campbell, Suzanne Miers, and Joseph C.
Miller (Athens: Ohio University Press, 2011), 221–37.

61. John Wall, "The Global Human Rights of Modern Child Slaves,"
in *When Is a Child a Slave? Child Slavery before and after Emancipa-
tion*, ed. Anna Mae Duane (New York: Cambridge University Press,
forthcoming).

62. Srikant Datar, Stacey Childress, Rachnna Tahilyani, and Anjali
Raina, "Pratham—Every Child in School and Learning Well" (case
study, Harvard Business School, 2010), accessed June 2015, http://api.
ning.com/files/.../Session9Pratham.pdf.

63. Asha Bajpai, *Child Rights in India: Law, Policy, and Practice*
(New York: Oxford University Press, 2003), 188–89.

64. Eric V. Edmonds and Nina Pavcnik, "Child Labor in the Global
Economy," *Journal of Economic Perspectives* 19, no. 1(2005): 199–220,
200.

65. Maggie Black, *Child Domestic Workers: A Handbook on Good
Practice in Programme Interventions*, Child Labour Series (London:
Anti-Slavery International, 2005), 17, 15 (respectively).

66. Patricia Ray, "The Participation of Children Living in the Poorest and Most Difficult Situations," in *A Handbook of Children and
Young People's Participation: Perspectives from Theory and Practice*,

ed. Barry Percey-Smith and Nigel Thomas (New York: Routledge, 2010), 61–72, 70.

67. Claire O'Kane, "Street Working Children's Participation in Programming for Their Rights," *Children, Youth and Environments* 13, no. 1 (Spring 2003): 167–83, 172–73.

68. Arjun Appadurai, *The Future as Cultural Fact: Essays on the Global Condition* (New York: Verso, 2013), 198.

6. THE RIGHT TO VOTE

1. John Wall, "Why Children and Youth Should Have the Right to Vote: An Argument for Proxy-Claim Suffrage," *Children, Youth and Environments* 24, no. 1 (2014): 108–23; Wall, "Democratizing Democracy: The Road from Women's to Children's Suffrage," in "A Renewed Call to Address Women's and Children's Human Rights," ed. Sonja Grover, special issue, *International Journal of Human Rights* 18, no. 6 (2014): 646–59; John Wall and Anandini Dar, "Children's Political Representation: The Right to Make a Difference," *International Journal of Children's Rights* 19, no. 4 (December 2011): 595–612.

2. See John Maddicott, *The Origins of the English Parliament, 924–1327* (Oxford: Oxford University Press; 2010); and Charles Seymour, *Electoral Reform in England and Wales* (Newton Abbott, UK: David & Charles Reprints, 1970).

3. Maree Brown and Jaleh McCormack, "Placing Children on the Political Agenda: New Zealand's Agenda for Children," in *The Politics of Childhood: International Perspectives, Contemporary Developments*, ed. Jim Goddard, Sally McNamee, Adrian James, and Allison James (New York: Palgrave Macmillan, 2005), 185–207.

4. Lucy Jamieson and Wanjiru Mukoma, "Dikwankwetla—Children in Action: Children's Participation in the Law Reform Process in South Africa," in *A Handbook of Children and Young People's Participation*, ed. Barry Percy-Smith and Nigel Thomas (New York: Routledge, 2010), 73–82.

5. Jen Williams and Rhian Croke, "Institutional Support for the UNCRC's 'Citizen Child,'" in *Children and Citizenship*, ed. Antonella Invernizzi and Jane Williams (Los Angeles: Sage, 2008), 184–87.

6. Asher Ben-Arieh and Yifat Boyer, "Citizenship and Childhood: The State of Affairs in Israel," *Childhood* 12, no. 1 (2005), 33–53, 50.

7. Ravi Karkara and Sultan Khudaibergenov, "National Adolescents and Youth Forum Held in Kazakhstan," UNICEF news release, 2009, http://www.unicef.kz.

8. Stefanie Conrad, "Children as Active Citizens: Addressing Discrimination against Children's Engagement in Political and Civil Society Processes," Plan International, 2009, https://plan-international.org; Sara L. Austin, "Children's Participation in Citizenship and Governance," in *A Handbook of Children and Young People's Participation*, ed. Barry Percy-Smith and Nigel Thomas (New York: Routledge, 2010), 245–53; Children's United Parliament of the World website, 2013, http://www.childrensstate.net; Stephanie McCrummen, "'Children's Parliament' Sets High Bar in Congo: Youthful Body in a Beacon of Justice," *Washington Post*, August 11, 2007; Neighborhood Community Network website, 2013, http://www.neighborhoodparliament.org; Jayashri Sarkar and Blanka Mendoza, "Bolivia's Children's Parliament: Bringing Participation to the National Stage," *Children, Youth and Environments* 15, no. 2 (2005): 227–44; Lalitha Sridhar, "Bal Sansads: Members of Parliament at 11," Infochange: News and Analysis of Social Justice and Development Issues in India, May 2004, http://infochangeindia.org/Bal-Sansads-Members-of-Parliament-at-11.html; Emma Williams, "Children's Participation and Policy Change in South Asia" (report, Save the Children, Childhood Poverty Research and Policy Centre, 2004), http://www.childhoodpoverty.org/index.php/action=documentfeed/doctype=pdf/id=86.

9. Alan Turkie, "More Than Crumbs from the Table: A Critique of Youth Parliaments as Models of Representation for Marginalised Young People," in *A Handbook of Children and Young People's Participation*, ed. Barry Percy-Smith and Nigel Thomas (New York: Routledge, 2010), 262–69; Michael Wyness, "Regulating Participation: The Possibilities and Limits of Children and Young People's Councils," in "Children's Citizenship: An Emergent Discourse on the Rights of the Child?," ed. A. Invernizzi and B. Milne, special issue, *Journal of Social Sciences*, no. 9 (2005): 7–18.

10. Mary John, *Children's Rights and Power: Charging Up for a New Century* (London: Jessica Kingsley, 2003), 235–39; Ahsa Bajpai, *Child*

Rights in India: Law, Policy, and Practice (New York: Oxford University Press, 2003), 469.

11. Yves Cabannes, "Children and Young People Build a Participatory Democracy in Latin American Cities," *Children, Youth and Environments* 15, no. 2 (2005): 185–210.

12. Sarkar and Mendoza, "Bolivia's Children's Parliament," 233–34.

13. Greg Hurst, "Ministers Contemplate Lowering the Voting Age to 16," *Times* (London), February 14, 2003.

14. BBC News, "Labour Conference: Ed Miliband Calls for Votes at 16," September 24, 2013, accessed September 25, 2013, http://www.bbc.co.uk/news/uk-politics-24229366.

15. Bobby Caina Calvan, "Californians Consider Granting 14-Year-Olds the Right to Vote," *Boston Globe*, April 25, 2004. See also the National Youth Rights Association website, http://www.youthrights.org.

16. CRIN (Children's Rights Information Network), "Germany: Children Should Have the Right to Vote, Say Parliamentarians," July 9, 2008, http://www.crin.org/resources/infoDetail.asp?ID=17831&flag=news; Harry De Quetteville, "Germany Plans to Give Vote to Babies," *Daily Telegraph*, July 9, 2008; Goethe Institute, "The Right to Vote from Birth On?," 2010, http://www.goethe.de/ges/pok/sup/en5570225.htm; and KRÄTZÄ (die KinderRÄchTsZÄnker) website, http://www.kraetzae.de.

17. Wall, "Democratizing Democracy: The Road from Women's to Children's Suffrage."

18. David Archard, *Children, Family and the State* (Burlington, VT: Ashgate, 2003), 53.

19. Benjamin R. Barber, "The Discourse of Civility," in *Citizen Competence and Democratic Institutions*, ed. Stephen L. Elkin and Karol E. Soltan (University Park: Pennsylvania State University Press, 1999), 39–47, 42–43.

20. John Rawls, *Political Liberalism* (New York: Columbia University Press, 1996), 245.

21. Jürgen Habermas, *Justification and Application: Remarks on Discourse Ethics*, trans. C. P. Cronin (Cambridge, MA: MIT Press, 1993), 64.

22. Daniel Hart and Robert Atkins, "American Sixteen- and Seventeen-Year-Olds Are Ready to Vote," *Annals of the American Academy of Political and Social Science* 633, no. 1 (2011): 201–22, 201. See also

Alex Folkes, "The Case for Votes at 16," *Representation* 41, no. 1 (2004): 52–56.

23. Hart and Atkins, "American Sixteen- and Seventeen-Year-Olds Are Ready to Vote," 220.

24. Bob Franklin, "Children's Political Rights," in *The Rights of Children* (New York: Basil Blackwell, 1986), 24–53, 34.

25. Francis Schrag, "Children and Democracy: Theory and Policy," *Politics, Philosophy and Economics* 3 (2004): 365–79, 371.

26. Claudio López-Guerra, *Democracy and Disenfranchisement: The Morality of Electoral Exclusions* (New York: Oxford University Press, 2014), 72.

27. López-Guerra, *Democracy and Disenfranchisement*, 78.

28. Charles C. Helwig, "The Moral Judgment of the Child Reevaluated: Heteronomy, Early Morality, and Reasoning about Social Justice and Inequalities," in *Social Development, Social Inequalities, and Social Justice*, ed. Cecilia Wainryb, Judith G. Smetana, and Elliot Turiel (New York: Erlbaum, 2008), 37.

29. Tak Wing Chan and Matthew Clayton, "Should the Voting Age Be Lowered to Sixteen? Normative and Empirical Considerations," *Political Studies* 54 (2006): 533–58, 542.

30. Philip Cowley and David Denver, "Votes at 16? The Case Against," *Representation* 41, no. 1 (2004): 57–62, 60.

31. John, *Children's Rights and Power*, 235–39.

32. Man-Yee Kan and Anthony Heath, "The Political Attitudes and Choices of Husbands and Wives" (working paper 103, Centre for Research into Elections and Social Trends [CREST]), 1–40, 3, http://www.crest.ox.ac.uk/papers/p103.pdf.

33. H. Elcock, "Young Voters 1988: Will They Break the Mold?" *Youth and Policy* 2, no. 2 (1983): 30–33.

34. Thomas Frank, *What's the Matter with Kansas? How Conservatives Won the Heart of America* (New York: Henry Holt, 2004).

35. Franklin, "Children's Political Rights," 36.

36. John Holt, *Escape from Childhood* (New York: Penguin, 1975), 155, 169.

37. Iris Marion Young, *Justice and the Politics of Difference* (Princeton, NJ: Princeton University Press, 1990), 120.

38. John Locke, *Two Treatises of Government*, rev. ed., ed. Peter Laslett (New York: Cambridge University Press, 1960), II.V.61 (309).

39. Geoffrey Scarre, "Children and Paternalism," *Philosophy* 55, no. 211 (1980): 117–24, 123.

40. Ludvig Beckman, *The Frontiers of Democracy: The Right to Vote and Its Limits* (New York: Palgrave Macmillan, 2009), 115.

41. Martin Guggenheim, *What's Wrong with Children's Rights* (Cambridge, MA: Harvard University Press, 2005), 266.

42. Franklin, "Children's Political Rights," 30–31.

43. Guggenheim, *What's Wrong with Children's Rights*, 13–14.

44. Cowley and Denver, "Votes at 16? The Case Against," 61.

45. Virginia Murphy-Berman, Helen L. Levesque, and John J. Berman, "U.N. Convention on the Rights of the Child: A Cross-Cultural View," *American Psychologist* 51, no. 12 (1996): 1257–61, 1259.

46. Cabannes, "Children and Young People Build a Participatory Democracy in Latin American Cities," 203.

47. Gayatri Chakravorty Spivak, "Can the Subaltern Speak?" in *Colonial Discourse and Postcolonial Theory: A Reader*, ed. Patrick Williams and Laura Chrisman (New York: Columbia University Press, 1994), 66–111.

7. TODAY'S GLOBAL CHALLENGE

1. Barbara Bennett Woodhouse, *Hidden in Plain Sight: The Tragedy of Children's Rights from Ben Franklin to Lionel Tate* (Princeton, NJ: Princeton University Press, 2008), 1–5.

INDEX

ABOUT THE AUTHOR

John Wall is professor of ethics and childhood studies at Rutgers University–Camden, where he specializes in ethical theory, post-modernity, and children's rights. His previous books include *Ethics in Light of Childhood* and *Moral Creativity* as well as the coedited volumes *Children and Armed Conflict, Marriage, Health, and the Professions,* and *Paul Ricoeur and Contemporary Moral Thought.* He is an award-winning teacher and lectures widely around the world to diverse audiences.

CPSIA information can be obtained at www.ICGtesting.com
Printed in the USA
BVOW08s0038011016

463870BV00002B/2/P